"America's leading source of self-help information." ★★★★

—YAHOO!

LEGAL INFORMATION ONLINE ANYTIME

24 hours a day

www.nolo.com

AT THE NOLO.COM SELF-HELP LAW CENTER, YOU'LL FIND

- Nolo's comprehensive Legal Encyclopedia filled with plain-English information on a variety of legal topics
- Nolo's Law Dictionary—legal terms <u>without</u> the legalese
- Auntie Nolo—if you've got questions, Auntie's got answers
- The Law Store—over 250 self-help legal products including: Downloadable Software, Books, Form Kits and eGuides
- Legal and product updates
- Frequently Asked Questions
- NoloBriefs, our free monthly email newsletter
- Legal Research Center, for access to state and federal statutes
- Our ever-popular lawyer jokes

Quality LAW BOOKS & SOFTWARE FOR EVERYONE

Nolo's user-friendly products are consistently first-rate. Here's why:

- A dozen in-house legal editors, working with highly skilled authors, ensure that our products are accurate, up-to-date and easy to use
- We continually update every book and software program to keep up with changes in the law
- Our commitment to a more democratic legal system informs all of our work
- We appreciate & listen to your feedback. Please fill out and return the card at the back of this book.

OUR "NO-HASSLE" GUARANTEE

Return anything you buy directly from Nolo for any reason and we'll cheerfully refund your purchase price. No ifs, ands or buts.

2nd edition

Domain Names

How to Choose & Protect a Great Name for Your Website

by Attorneys Stephen Elias
and Patricia Gima

KEEPING UP-TO-DATE

To keep its books up-to-date, Nolo issues new printings and new editions periodically. New printings reflect minor legal changes and technical corrections. New editions contain major legal changes, major text additions or major reorganizations. To find out if a later printing or edition of any Nolo book is available, call Nolo at 510-549-1976 or check our website at http://www.nolo.com.

To stay current, follow the "Update" service at our website at www.nolo.com/update. In another effort to help you use Nolo's latest materials, we offer a 35% discount off the purchase of the new edition of your Nolo book when you turn in the cover of an earlier edition. This book was last revised in May 2001.

SECOND EDITION	**May 2001**
EDITOR	Lisa Sedano
PROOFREADER	Robert Wells
INDEXER	Ellen Davenport
COVER	Toni Ihara
PRINTING	Consolidated Printers, Inc.

Elias, Stephen.
   Domain names : how to choose and protect a great name for your website / by Stephen
Elias and Patricia Gima.-- 2nd ed.
     p. cm.
  Includes index.
  ISBN 0-87337-761-3
  1. Internet domain names. I. Gima, Patricia. II. Title.
  TK5105.875.I57 .E43 2001
  004.6'78--dc21   2001030464

Quantity sales: For information on bulk purchases or corporate premium sales, please contact the Special Sales department. For academic sales or textbook adoptions, ask for Academic Sales, 800-955-4775, Nolo, 950 Parker St., Berkeley, CA 94710.

ACKNOWLEDGMENTS

Thanks to Patti Gima, my wonderful co-author, and to Mary Randolph for her marvelous editing and ever-cheerful support for this book. Thanks also to the many wonderful folks at Nolo who keep the Nolo flame burning bright and bring our goods to market.

DEDICATIONS

To Rubin Santiago Elias, a good friend, great son and true child of the Internet.

—Steve Elias

ACKNOWLEDGMENTS

Many thanks to my husband, Joe, and my sons, Jordan and Asher, for their unwavering support. Thank you, Mary Randolph, for your precision editing. Thanks, Steve Elias, for being a great co-author. Thanks, too, to Terri Hearsh for the swift and wonderful book layout.

DEDICATION

I'd like to dedicate this book (or my portion of it) to Jordan, Asher and Joe. Three constant sources of creativity.

—Patricia Gima

Contents

CHAPTER 4

HOW TO CHOOSE A GREAT DOMAIN NAME

CHAPTER 5

WHAT TO DO IF YOUR DOMAIN NAME IS ALREADY TAKEN

CHAPTER 6

MAKING SURE YOUR DOMAIN NAME DOESN'T CONFLICT WITH ANOTHER BUSINESS'S TRADEMARK

CHAPTER 7

HOW TO TELL WHETHER CUSTOMER CONFUSION IS LIKELY

CHAPTER 8

HOW TO REGISTER YOUR DOMAIN NAME AS A TRADEMARK

CHAPTER 9

HELP BEYOND THIS BOOK

APPENDICES

APPENDIX A: GLOSSARY

APPENDIX B: INTERNATIONAL SCHEDULE OF CLASSES OF
GOODS AND SERVICES

APPENDIX C: IDENTIFICATION AND CLASSIFICATION OF CERTAIN
COMPUTER-RELATED GOODS AND SERVICES

INDEX

Icons Used in This Book

 Caution: A potential problem.

 See an Expert: An instance when you may need the advice of an attorney or other expert.

 Tip: A bit of advice that may help you with a particular issue.

 Resources: Books, websites or other resources that may be of use.

 Fast Track: Lets you know that you may be able to skip some material.

KEEPING UP TO DATE

The world of domain names is changing as fast as the Internet itself, but books are difficult to keep up-to-date between editions. We'll post significant new developments in the Updates section of http://www.nolo.com. Checking there should keep you current.

The Legal Side of Domain Names

To do business on the Web, you'll need at least one domain name— the yada-yada-dot-com that has become so familiar in commercials and print advertising. Your domain name may be the name you already use for a business, with a dot-com added, or a new name that you think will do a good job of getting people to your website. If you follow the lead of many businesses, you'll use multiple domain names to help the widest possible number of potential customers find your site among the many thousands out there.

Choosing a name, or more than one, for your website is no trivial matter—your decisions can make or break your business. This explains why some domain names have been auctioned off for huge amounts of money. The current record-holder is business.com, which went for an astounding $7.5 million. The winning bidder apparently believes the name has enough customer-drawing power to make it worthwhile. Fortunately for small e-commerce start-ups with limited budgets, most businesses make up their domain names or use names that they are already using as trademarks, and don't pay anyone a penny for the privilege.

DOMAIN NAME ANATOMY

Domain names consist of two main parts: the top-level domain name, or TLD, and the second-level domain name, or SLD. The SLD comes first, and it is the part that makes your domain name unique. For example, in nolo.com, nolo is the SLD.

The TLD comes at the end of the domain name, after the ubiquitous dot. TLDs are organized, for U.S. participants, into five categories:

- .com, for commercial groups
- .edu, for educational institutions
- .gov, for governmental entities
- .org, for nonprofit organizations, and
- .net, for interactive discussion groups.

Other countries have their own TLDs—for example, .fr for France, .gr for Greece, .to for Tonga.

Almost all U.S. businesses choose to operate under the .com domain. On November 16, 2000, ICANN (the International Corporation for Assigned Names and Numbers), the international body responsible for domain name issues, announced that seven new TLDs will be available in 2001. These are:

- .aero, for the air-transport industry
- .biz, for businesses
- .coop, for non-profit cooperatives
- .info, for unrestricted use
- .museum, for museums
- .name, for registration by individuals, and
- .pro, for accountants, lawyers and physicians.

Even so, most businesses will still choose to be "dotcoms."

A. Thinking About the Law

You may have thought a lot about the marketing aspects of your domain name—how the name can attract visitors, communicate what you do, stick in customers' minds and inspire confidence in your business. All those factors definitely deserve attention, but there's another set of concerns that is at least as important: how trademark law affects your choice and use of a name.

If your domain name is the same as or similar to a trademark already being used by a competing or related business, that business might force you to stop using it somewhere down the road. And if you have built up considerable goodwill under the domain name when a trademark conflict flares up, this could amount to a business catastrophe. You can avoid this potential disaster by picking a domain name that is free and clear from legal conflicts.

IF SOMEONE CHALLENGES YOUR DOMAIN NAME

This book is not designed to help you if your existing domain name comes under legal attack—for instance, if another business demands that you surrender your domain name. If that happens, we recommend *Trademark: Legal Care for Your Product & Service Name*, by Stephen Elias (Nolo), or to Nolo's downloadable eGuide, *Trademark Disputes: Who Wins, Who Loses & Why*. You may also need to consult a lawyer.

Some names are wonderful from a commercial perspective but close enough to existing names to cause a legal tiff, such as the dispute between etoys.com, a large toy dealer, and etoy.com, a small website created by Swiss artists. Still other names may be unique as domain names but identical or confusingly similar to names used by brick-and-mortar-companies—a fact which easily can give rise to a trademark infringement lawsuit.

Fortunately, you can select a domain name that will be both commercially appropriate for your business and free from legal challenges by other businesses. Your best strategy may be to leverage your existing business name, with strong customer recognition, by using it (or part of it) as your domain name. But if you're just starting out, you may want to invent something catchy and different.

B. Protecting the Name You Choose

To be sure that your name really is different—not identical to or similar enough to someone else's trademarked name to cause a problem—you need to search for available domain names and register your domain name with a domain name registry service. The next step is to file an application with the U.S. Patent and Trademark Office to register your domain name as a trademark.

STEPS IN CHOOSING AND RESERVING A DOMAIN NAME

☐ If you've picked out a domain name, reserve it so it won't get snapped up by another business. (Chapter 2)

☐ If you haven't yet chosen a domain name, select one that will get people to your website and also qualify for protection as a trademark. (Chapters 3 and 4)

☐ If your preferred name is taken, consider alternate names and your legal options. (Chapter 5)

☐ Use the Internet to search for existing trademarks that legally conflict with your name. (Chapters 6 and 7)

☐ If your name conflicts with an existing trademark, choose another name (Chapter 4) or, if you are already using the name as a mark, assert your rights as a trademark owner. (Chapter 5)

☐ For maximum protection for your name, apply for federal trademark registration. (Chapter 8)

■

How to Reserve a Domain Name

If you've already chosen a domain name, your first step should be to register it with a domain name registration service. This will give you the exclusive right to use that domain name.

You may want to register a name—or more than one—even if you haven't yet searched for possible trademark conflicts (see Chapter 6) or made a final decision about your domain name. Websites are going up in great numbers, and if you wait, you may lose the name you want. You risk wasting the amount of the reservation or registration fee if you later decide to use a different name. But that risk may be worth it if you ultimately decide to use your first choice and you've managed to prevent someone else from grabbing it first.

Example: *Geoff wants to use the domain name doctortrademark.com for his website, which offers legal advice on trademarks. He checks the availability of that name and learns that it has been taken. Geoff then checks drtrademark.com and finds that it's available. Although Geoff knows (because he has read Chapter 7) that using such a similar domain name might infringe the doctortrademark.com trademark, he decides to go ahead and reserve the name until he can do some more investigation regarding the other "Doctor Trademark" website.*

If the exact domain name you want has been taken by someone else, you will not be able to register it unless you have already been using the name as a trademark and are willing to take the steps described in Chapter 5 to assert your legal rights as a trademark owner.

⚠ Don't be a cybersquatter. It is against federal law to register someone else's personal or business name as your domain name, if you're doing it because you want to sell the name back to its owner for a profit.

If you are choosing a domain name for the purpose of using it on a website that will be doing legitimate commerce, you have nothing to worry about. However, if you are buying up domain names so you can sell them later, you should definitely get some advice from a lawyer about the legality of your activity. The federal Anti-Cybersquatting Consumer Protection Act, which prohibits cybersquatting, and ICANN's dispute resolution procedures are discussed in detail in Chapter 5.

A. Where to Register

An increasingly large number of domain name registration agencies have been accredited by ICANN. A list of these agencies and a brief description of each is available on the ICANN website at http://www.icann.org. All of these agencies use a shared central registry, maintained by Network Solutions, Inc. (NSI), to ensure that duplicate addresses are not issued.

After checking the availability of your name with one of these agencies, you can reserve it with a credit card. If you want to register the name right then and there, you must be prepared to give the agency information about your Internet Service Provider and who will be hosting (physically maintaining) your website.

A WORD ABOUT NSI

Until mid-1999, NSI was the only U.S. registration agency. While there are now a slew of additional registration agencies, NSI is still the largest and has the most experience. For this reason and for the sake of convenience, the registration examples throughout this book usually reference NSI. However, that should not prevent you from exploring other registration agencies, many of which offer both registration and other related services at varying prices.

B. How to Check the Availability of and Register a Domain Name

All of the domain name registries offer a combination of services designed to help you search for available domain names and reserve or register names that interest you. Either on (or through) the registries' websites, you can:

- search the domain name database to see whether your proposed name is available (free)
- obtain a list of related names that are available instead of, or in addition to, your proposed name (free)
- register or reserve a domain name for a one, two, five or ten year period (an approximate cost of $35 a year)
- search ownership information about existing domain names (free), and
- sign up with an affiliate service for fee-based Web creation and hosting services.

To see how this works, let's take a look at the NSI website at http://www.nsi.com.

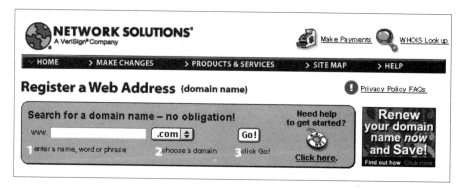

Figure 1

Figure 1 shows NSI's home page. To use this site to find out whether a domain name is available,

- enter your proposed name in the "Register a Web Address" box
- select the TLD you want (probably .com), and
- click the go button.

The results of the search tell you whether your proposed name is available and suggest other names that you may also wish to register. For instance, when the authors searched for "selfhelplawproject.com," we learned that this particular name is not available but that other names were. Figure 2 shows our results.

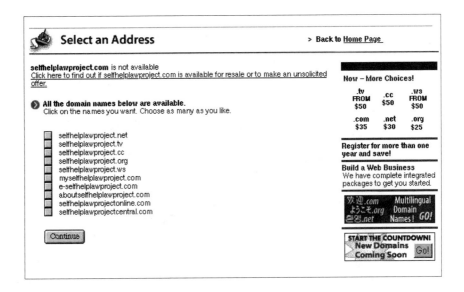

Figure 2

![warning icon] **Be careful about choosing a close alternate name.** In Chapter 4, we point out that choosing a name that is close to an existing domain name may get you into trademark trouble. Also, you could be forced to surrender the name under the ICANN domain name dispute resolution policy.

If we check the box before "selfhelplawproject.net" and click "continue," we will then be offered a series of options, as shown in Figure 3:

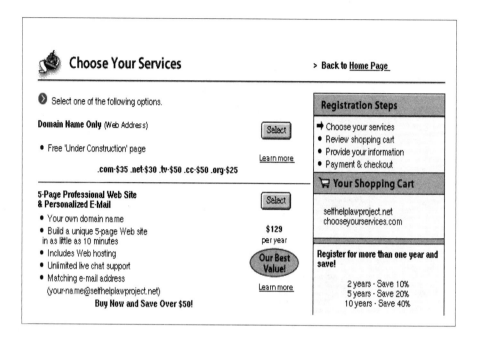

Figure 3

To secure a domain name, select the first option. This gives you a choice between reserving your name for $40 a year or registering it for $35 a year. If you register the name, you need to give NSI technical information about your ISP and website host. If you spend the extra money to just reserve the name, you can provide this information at a later date.

When you decide to either register or reserve the name, you will see another page that asks you to select the number of years you want to pay for. After that, you will be asked for some personal and credit card information.

If your name is taken, you may be interested in searching the WHOIS database at http://www.whois.net. Here, you can find information about the registrant of any domain name. Say, for example, you have chosen *Webvan, Inc.*, as the name of your grocery delivery business and want to use webvan.com as your domain name. However, you soon discover that someone else has already taken this domain name. You run the name through the WHOIS search engine and find that Intelligent Systems for Retail, Inc., is the domain name registrant. The search results also give you a contact name, phone number, address and email address. From there, you can decide whether you want to contact Intelligent Systems for Retail, Inc., perhaps to make an offer to buy the name. (Chapter 5 discusses more options if your chosen name is not available.)

C. What to Register

In addition to your product or service name, you may want to register one or more related names, if they are available. These might be common misspellings of the primary name, names of specific product brands owned by your business and names that reflect the generic nature of your products. For instance, *Peet's Coffee & Tea* owns not only peets.com, but also coffee.com. Peet's might want to lock up petes.com (for the bad spellers), petescoffee.com and peetscoffee.com. (See Chapter 4 for more on how to choose a great domain name.) ■

When Your Domain Name Is a Trademark

If you are doing e-business on your website, or using the website to advertise goods or services you offer in the "real world," your domain name is also a trademark. Simply put, a trademark is any device that distinguishes your product or service from others in the marketplace, or designates their origin. For instance, say Jonah Ishmael creates an online art gallery that features and sells whale art by various artists. The art gallery is called *Jonah and the Whale* and resides on a website with the domain name ahab.com. Jonah is using ahab.com as a trademark because it is used to bring visitors to his commercially oriented website. Jonah is also using *Jonah and the Whale* as a trademark for the particular product being offered on the website—whale art.

Here are some examples of domain names that are also trademarks:

- Amazon.com (online retailer of books, CDs, toys and other items)
- Drugstore.com (online pharmaceuticals sales)
- Nolo.com (online legal information provider and publisher and retailer of legal books, forms and software).

A domain name isn't always a trademark. If ahab.com were a personal, noncommercial website with pictures of Jonah's family, poems he writes from time to time and a statement of his political philosophy, the domain name would not be a trademark. This is because the term ahab wouldn't be used to identify goods or services or an entity doing business on or off the Web.

Also, if a domain name is the same name by which the product or service is typically described, the law will consider it "generic" and won't treat it as a trademark. For instance, the domain name drugs.com uses a word that is the generic term for a class of products. As we point out in more detail in Chapter 4, generic names like drugs.com may make fabulous domain names but will most likely never receive protection as a trademark because the law does not allow monopolies over generic terms.

A. Your Rights As a Trademark Owner

Why should you care whether or not your domain name is a trademark? Because as the owner of a trademark, you have legal rights that are important to your business. If you're the first person or business to actually use a particular trademark in connection with the sale of goods or services, you are the "senior user" of that mark and you have priority in case of a conflict with a later user. This is true whether or not you've registered the trademark with the U.S. Patent and Trademark Office.

Example: *Peter develops software for taking orders over the Web and launches the sale of his Bearware software online. He uses the mark Bearware prominently on his website and as his domain name, bearware.com. Peter makes his software available for purchase online under the mark Bearware and through the domain name bearware.com on February 1, 2000, so that is the date of first use for purposes of trademark seniority. Gail develops similar software and also plans to market it under the trademark and domain name Bearware.com. But Gail doesn't offer her software for sale until March 1, 2000.*

Because Peter was the first to use the mark Bearware to sell his software, he is the senior user. If Gail sues him for trademark infringement, he will win the right to continue using the mark for selling his software and as his domain name.

If you're the senior user, you can go to court to prevent others from using your trademark or a similar trademark—as a domain name or otherwise—if the use would likely cause customers to confuse the other product or service with yours, or to be confused as to the origin of the product or service. (See Chapter 7 for more on what constitutes customer confusion.)

Example: *Gail decides to sell her software under the Bearware mark over the Internet, but she uses the domain name bareware.com. Peter can sue Gail for trademark infringement, asking the court to stop Gail from using the*

*Bearware mark and the barewear.com domain name. Peter will make a
number of claims:*

1. *He is the senior user of the mark Bearware.*

2. *Gail's use of the same mark to market and sell her software product
   (which is similar to Peter's) and her use of a domain name that
   sounds exactly like Peter's trademark are likely to cause customers
   to confuse her product and website with Peter's.*

3. *Gail's use of the same mark as Peter's for a similar software application is likely to cause customers to mistakenly believe that both
   applications come from the same company.*

B. Trademark Registration

Trademark ownership in the United States is based on who is first to use
the mark (the senior user). But you can strengthen your claim to ownership by registering a mark with the United States Patent and Trademark
Office. This also applies to domain names that serve as trademarks—that
is, domain names that are used as addresses for commercial websites.
Generally, you can federally register a trademark if it is:

- used in interstate or international commerce (which includes
  virtually all commercial domain names)

- not a generic term (a term which describes an entire class or
  group of goods or services)

- not scandalous or immoral (four-letter words are verboten),
  and

- not likely to create customer confusion when compared with
  other registered marks.

The primary benefits of federal registration are that you are presumed
to be the owner of the mark throughout the whole country, and anyone
who infringes your mark will be presumed to have done it willfully.

The presumptions can be rebutted in court with evidence to the
contrary; for example, if your opponent shows he used the mark before

you did, your claim of ownership may fail. By putting the burden on your opponent, however, these presumptions are quite powerful and a real benefit. If you prove infringement occurred, you can collect large money damages, and possibly attorneys' fees in a federal lawsuit. Also, you are entitled to use the "r in a circle" notation next to your name to inform the world of your mark ownership. Unregistered marks are identified with the less powerful "™."

Chapter 8 explains the rules and benefits of registration in more detail and provides step-by-step instructions for filing a registration application online.

 For a more complete treatment of these and other trademark issues, see *Trademark: Legal Care for Your Business & Product Name,* by Stephen Elias (Nolo), or visit the Patent, Copyright and Trademark section of Nolo's free Legal Encyclopedia at www.nolo.com.

PROTECTION FOR UNREGISTERED TRADEMARKS

State Trademark Registration Laws. You can register your trademark with your state, but there are few practical benefits. State registrations were more important when it was common for marks to be used solely within a single state, which meant they didn't qualify for federal registration. However, with the advent of the Internet, very few marks are now restricted to a state's geographical borders, and federal registration is definitely the preferred approach.

State and Federal Unfair Competition Laws. Trademarks that have not been federally registered can still receive certain kinds of limited protection under state and federal unfair competition laws. These laws bar other businesses from using your trademark in confusing and unfair ways. Protection from unfair competition is most useful when another business is trying to use your trademark to create the impression that its business is affiliated with yours. In other words, unfair competition laws can help you if someone isn't making it clear that they are not connected to your business.

For more on unfair competition, see *Trademark: Legal Care for Your Business & Product Name,* by Stephen Elias (Nolo).

C. Making a Domain Name a Strong Trademark

A distinctive domain name gets more legal protection as a trademark than a non-distinctive one does, and is usually more effective in the marketplace. The law grants distinctive domain names used as trademarks greater power to ward off copiers, for three reasons:

Distinctive names are memorable. The more distinctive a trademark is, like Yahoo!, the greater impression it makes on the customer's memory. This strong impression makes it more likely that a similar trademark, say Yoohoo.com used as a Web portal, will remind the customer of the original trademark. Needless to say, that can lead to confusion. Customers may think Yahoo! and Yoohoo are the same brand, or that they are related. They may mistakenly type in yoohoo.com instead of yahoo.com and go to the wrong website. They may be misled into thinking the reputation of one applies to the other. In either case, the rightful owner of the Yahoo! trademark may lose traffic, ad sales and profits.

Similar names are likely to confuse customers. The more distinctive a domain name is, the more likely it is that potential customers will assume that all products and services carrying that name originate from one source. For instance, it's reasonable to assume that all insurance-related services that carry the QuoteSmith mark, as in Quotesmith.com, originate from one company called QuoteSmith. You wouldn't make the same assumption for several quote services that use "value" in their names. The greater the likelihood that customers will associate a product or service carrying a particular name with a particular source, the greater the need to protect them against the confusion that would likely result if another business used the same or a similar name.

The business probably invested time and money to come up with the name. The more time, money and creativity that go into making a domain name distinctive, the more sense it makes to provide the mark with adequate protection. And if the distinctiveness comes from widespread customer recognition over time, it also makes sense to protect the business good-will that has been built up under the mark.

To come up with a domain name that will serve you well as a trademark, follow these rules:

1. Use a name that's memorable or clever.
2. If you use a name that isn't distinctive, promote it so that it acquires a meaning in the marketplace.
3. Avoid conflicts with names that are already famous.

These strategies are discussed in Chapter 4. ■

How to Choose a Great Domain Name

To help your e-business flourish, you want to pick a domain name that will:

- be easy for web searchers to find
- help market your product or service
- serve as a strong trademark, so competitors won't be able to use it or something similar, and
- be free of legal conflicts with other trademarks.

This chapter explores strategies for meeting these sometimes contradictory goals.

A. One Website, Many Domain Names

It's an unfortunate but inescapable fact that a domain name that satisfies one of the goals listed above may sabotage another. For example, a domain name that gets lots of people to your website quickly may make a crummy trademark. Take coffee.com; it may be an excellent domain name, because many people who are looking for coffee vendors online are likely to type the word coffee into their browsers. But coffee.com wouldn't qualify as a trademark for a coffee-related website, because the word coffee in that context is generic—it describes the product itself. So if your website were named coffee.com, you wouldn't be able to do much about goodcoffee.com, blackcoffee.com, columbiancoffee.com or cupofcoffee.com. But if you named your coffee website something like javadelights.com, you would have an easier time of chasing away anything that was similar in sight, sound or meaning. Coffee.com or javadelights.com? What a choice.

Fortunately, you can have the best of both worlds—you can claim several domain names and route them all to a single website. In fact, you can have an unlimited number of domain names leading to your unique website. This is because underneath every website lurks a set of numbers (your Internet Protocol, or IP, address) that identifies your unique location on a particular Internet server. Your Internet service provider can set up a system that routes multiple domain names to your IP address, and so to your website.

The only factor limiting how many domain names you can use to bring users to your particular website is cost. Registration costs about $35 per year, so registering ten domain names would cost only $350, a modest amount for many Internet startups.

Because Internet users vary in how they seek out goods, services and established businesses online, the more bases you cover the better. So the owners of a coffee-related website might, as an example, register cupofcoffee.com, coffeeyumyum.com and cupofjoe.com as well as javadelights.com.

Another way to leverage a domain name is to create variations by adding words to the front of it, with another dot. For example, if you were using www.jelly.com and wanted to promote the New England jams and jellies you were selling, you could also use www.Vermont.jelly.com, www.Maine.jelly.com or NewEngland.jelly.com and so on, without registering additional domain names. These domain names could link to specific parts of your website; your ISP could set it up for you.

You're free to create as many variations like this as you can think of. Just be sure to add another dot when you add to the name. The domain name www.Vermontjelly.com (without the dot after "Vermont") would be a completely different domain name from www.jelly.com, and you would have to register it separately.

A potential downside to this strategy is that some folks may forget to include the extra dots when entering your domain name in their browser, and as a result will be taken to a different site or get a "no server found" message. If they take the time to error-check, though, they should be able to figure it out.

CHECK FOR BULK DISCOUNTS

Some domain name registries offer discounts for bulk domain name registrations. For example, http://nameit.net offers registration of between 50 and 299 domain names for $9.49 per year per name. If you plan on registering a large number of names, it will be worth your while to shop around. A list of accredited domain name registrars is available at http://www.icann.org.

B. If You're Already in Business

If you are launching a website as part of an existing business, you must first decide whether you want to use the name of your business for at least one of your domain names. Most businesses do. That's why you'll find apple.com, landsend.com, toysrus.com and so on.

The importance of a strong brand on the Internet can't be overstated. Strong national and global competition for products and services online demands strong branding and a correlation between brand and domain name in order to get customers to the right website.

For example, say you are looking for the website of Peet's Coffee & Tea, a well-known coffee supplier. Rather than use a search engine to hunt for sites related to the terms "coffee" or "tea," you probably would first just type "peets.com" into your browser. Your guess would be right, and you would go right to the Peet's website. Had Peet's not used its brand name for its domain name, you would have been at least temporarily diverted from your search. And if you share the general lack of patience of many Internet users, you might have given up. By using its strong brand name for its domain name, Peet's can rest assured that anyone looking for the brand will quickly end up at its website.

Using the company name for your domain name also allows you to keep whatever goodwill you have built in the name. Goodwill simply means the good relationship you have with your customers because you provide exceptional service or a truly wonderful product.

You may decide, however, that a short, catchy and easy-to-remember name is a good alternative (or addition) to just using your existing business name. For example, the Collin Street Bakery in Corsicana, Texas, sells fruitcakes and has for many years—but when it came time to go online, the owners chose fruitcake.com as their domain name.

Still another option is to use only part of your business name, or an abbreviated form of it, as your domain name. For example, Turners Outdoorsman, (retail sporting goods) uses turners.com; Motley Fool (investment advice) uses fool.com, and Kelley Blue Book (wholesale and retail prices for used cars) is kbb.com. Ask Jeeves, a well-known search engine, uses ask.com. Short domain names are generally preferable to long ones, because many Internet users type the domain names into their browsers rather than relying on their list of favorite or bookmarked sites, portals (Yahoo!, AOL), or special interest sites that offer collections of links for parents, seniors, investors or other groups.

Of course, you may want to use another name altogether (like the bakery that chose fruitcake.com), especially if your business name is long. For instance, a well-known bookstore chain in Northern California called A Clean Well-Lighted Place for Books uses bookstore.com as its domain name.

As mentioned, generic domain names make weak trademarks because they merely describe the goods or services offered on the website (for example, healthanswers.com, drugstore.com, coffee.com), but excellent domain names because they work to get people to the website. So, depending on how well known your existing business name is, it may make sense to use two names. Create a new and descriptive domain name, and use your existing business name both as a second domain name and to sell goods or services on the website itself. The rest of this chapter gives more tips on choosing a good name.

C. Generic Names

A generic term can make a great domain name, because lots of people are likely to find your site. That's why domain names such as wine.com, furniture.com, pets.com and books.com were snapped up long ago. Of course, as the demise of pets.com shows, a generic name doesn't ensure that the many people who find your site will actually buy anything there.

As a general rule, generic domain names work best when you can use the actual term without modifiers or additional syllables. For instance, cars.com, drugs.com or coffee.com are the strongest and best uses of these generic terms. Domain names like fastcars.com, coffeebeans.com or bestdrugs.com aren't going to bring as many people to your site as the bare term would, but they're still considered generic for trademark purposes, meaning you get the worst of both worlds—an ineffective domain name and no trademark protection, either. If someone has got there ahead of you and is already using a key term by itself, consider adopting a classically distinctive domain name—that is, a name that is coined, arbitrary, fanciful, suggestive or flat-out clever. (See Section E, below.)

If you're considering a generic domain name (and someone else hasn't grabbed it yet), think it over before you decide to go with that name alone. As mentioned, having a generic name can certainly make it easier for people to find you on the Web. But because the name is generic, you probably will not have any trademark protection, and the U.S. Patent and Trademark Office probably won't register it. If you want to register your domain name as a national trademark, it must be distinctive enough to distinguish your product or service from others in the marketplace. For example, if a business names its new soft drink "Cola" and its website cola.com, it won't be able to register "cola" as a trademark and it won't be able to stop another company from using the term. That's because "cola" describes a group of carbonated soft drinks with cola flavoring; it could refer to any of several brands of colas. But add "Shasta" to "Cola," and shastacola.com qualifies as a trademark because it specifies one particular brand of cola on the market. Other examples of terms that have always been generic are lite beer, super glue, softsoap, matchbox cars and supermarket.

D. Ordinary or Common Names

Many excellent domain names are made up of ordinary words. Consider taxprophet.com. Nothing remarkable about either tax or prophet, but put them together and you have a name with considerable cachet. Another example, Webvan.com, is the website of a grocery delivery service. There is nothing unusual about the words, but their combination is clever because it makes you wonder what is being delivered and piques your curiosity.

But what about trademark protection for a name consisting of ordinary terms? Here are the basic rules:

- If the overall name is distinctive, it will be protected as a trademark no matter how many ordinary terms are used.

- You cannot claim ownership to the ordinary terms themselves, but only to the overall name. For example, the owner of howstuffworks.com won't own "how" or "stuff" or "works," but will own the entire name.

- If the ordinary terms are memorable in the context of the product or service (for instance, Apple in the context of computers), the name is said to have acquired "secondary meaning." Common terms that consumers have come, over time, to associate with the underlying product or service have acquired secondary meaning—for example, bestbuy.com for retail electronic products.

1. The General Rule: Little Legal Protection

On a scale of one to ten for trademark protection, generic names rate a zero, while distinctive names are a ten. In between are all sorts of names that aren't usually distinctive by themselves, but aren't generic either. This "ordinary names" category includes:

- names that use common terms in a standard arrangement—for example, healthanswers.com for, you guessed it, online health information
- place names such as DowntownNews.com
- personal names—for example, www.troweprice.com for T. Rowe Price investment funds; castlelaw.com for the Castleman Law Firm
- words that describe the product or service, such as i-courthouse.com for an online court that resolves disputes and allows Internet participants to serve as jurors; stampfinders.com, a full-service exchange for stamp collectors, and
- words of praise, such as bestpetshop.com (unless it becomes well-known over time, as in bestbuys.com).

Misspellings or alternative spellings (such as "lite") cannot make an ordinary term ("light") distinctive. The same is true for common foreign language equivalents, like "le" for "the" and "casa" for "house." As a result, bestpetshop.com predictably will get little legal protection as a trademark. By contrast, a fanciful domain name like petopia.com is distinctive and easily protected as a trademark.

2. Protection If the Name Becomes Well-Known

If an ordinary name becomes associated in the public mind with a product or service, the name becomes entitled to strong trademark protection. This is called the "secondary meaning" rule. Many famous and effective trademarks, like McDonald's or The Yellow Pages, originally consisted of ordinary terms that, over time, became widely recognized as product and service identifiers and so were transformed into strong marks. From its humble beginning as an ordinary mark, McDonald's has turned into one of the strongest marks in the world.

Similarly, when it first hit the market, the name Ben & Jerry's for a brand of ice cream was not associated with a particular product and not entitled to much protection. However, as the Ben & Jerry's company advertised its products and as the products became well known (actually, adored) among the nation's ice cream buffs, the Ben & Jerry's trademark became associated with high quality ice cream. Now, the mark has strong recognition as a brand of upscale ice cream—and the company's website is named, of course, benandjerrys.com. Other examples include schwab.com for investment services, Christies.com for auctions, sportingnews.com for the well-known sports periodical, and etrade.com for online stock trading. Marks such as these which have acquired secondary meaning are said to have acquired "distinctiveness."

Using a mark that can't be protected until it has acquired a secondary meaning can present a serious problem to your small business. You must accept the fact that the mark will be weak, and subject to possible use by others, until its reputation has been built up. If you can spend a lot of money to promote the mark when it's first used, you may be able to speed up the process of public recognition.

E. Distinctive Names

Memorable domain names can make a strong impression on customers and are legally strong trademarks, easier to protect against use by others than generic or ordinary names. They make customers think, "That's clever," or "Gee, I wonder what that means?" A product or service name can be distinctive for a number of reasons, including:

- The name is coined (made up)—for example, flooz.com, datek.com or multex.com.

- The combination of words and letters in the name is so creative that no one else has come up with it—for example, vineswinger.com for virtual winery tours and wine mail-order services.

- The name carries a clever double meaning—for example, the name of google.com, an online search engine, is based on "googol," a word used by mathematicians for the number ten raised to the power of 100. Another example: a bioinformation company, uses doubletwist.com for its domain name, suggesting the famous double-helix structure of DNA.

- Certain words in the name are completely arbitrary in the context of the underlying product or service, as in online retailer Amazon.com; rhino.com, the website of Rhino Records; fool.com, the site for the Motley Fool investment advice firm and dogpile.com for search services.

- The name as a whole cleverly suggests the product without describing it, as in lendingtree.com for loans, hungryminds.com for online education, magicaldesk.com for secretarial services, medscape.com for health services and bottomdollar.com for a shopping site.

Marks such as these are said to be "inherently distinctive," as opposed to those that have become distinctive by acquiring secondary meaning.

F. Creating a Distinctive Domain Name

George Eastman, the founder of Kodak and a man with an eye for a good trademark, could have been talking about domain names when he suggested that trademarks should:

- be short
- be vigorous

- be easily spelled, and

- mean nothing.

Some other good advice is to make your domain name:

- pronounceable

- memorable, and

- legally available (see Chapter 5).

The key to creating a distinctive domain name is cleverness. Coined words such as Exxon are the ultimate in clever because they are created from thin air. But you don't need to make up new words to have a distinctive name. As we have seen, distinctive names often consist of ordinary words used creatively and in an unusual context or words that evoke fanciful associations. You may also want to use ordinary words that indirectly suggest what the underlying product or service is, without describing it outright.

While it may seem that all the good names have been taken, there is in fact a large supply. But like diamonds, they usually aren't just lying on the ground for the taking; a little mining, cutting and polishing may be required to find them and make them shine. Some possible sources:

- new combinations of existing words such as ubid.com for auctions, smartmoney.com for personal finance calculators, buyitnow.com for a retail site

- combinations of word roots, like intelihealth.com for health services, bibliofind.com or alibris.com for book finding services, travelocity.com for travel services, invesco.com for investment services

- distinctive foreign words such as Sirocco.com or Soleil.com

- abandoned names that are no longer in use, but that were once famous. They may bring a certain cachet to your product or service if their image corresponds to the one you want to project. If you do discover a name you know was in use at one time, find out whether or not it is now available for your use by doing the sort of search described in Chapter 6.

FINDING UNCLAIMED MARKS

One online subscription service claims to have an inside track to domain names that were not renewed after their two-year registration expired. The service provides a list of these recently expired registrations on a weekly basis for a $20 subscription fee. While we don't endorse this service or provide any guarantees, such a list might provide a fruitful source of domain name ideas. You can reach the service at www.unclaimeddomains.com.

If you do decide to use one of the names on this list, make sure that the name isn't still being used as a trademark on or off the Web. As with other domain name choices you may make, you should definitely subject your choice to a trademark search, as described in Chapter 6.

1. Fanciful Marks

The best way to make a mark distinctive is to make it up. Some examples include chumbo.com (an online software store), kagi.com (a payment processing service for e-commerce businesses) and pandesic.com (an e-commerce company). The keys to a coined (or "fanciful") trademark are making it easy to spell and appealing to both eye and ear, or at least suitable to the image you want to project for your product or service. To avoid coined words that may evoke unintended images (for example, runslo.com for software that is supposed to speed up your Internet access), run your choices by a variety of people and note their responses to the sound and appearance.

Wholly new, made-up words have no meaning and probably not even any connotation, other than the ones you will create with your marketing activities. That means they require extensive, often expensive, marketing efforts to get established as product or service identifiers in the first place. Without that, your domain name won't mean anything to the general public. That's a major drawback for a small business with limited capital.

Opting for a fanciful mark has a second drawback. New combinations that sound and look good—that is, ones that are marketable and not already in use—are becoming harder to develop. Despite our rich Celtic, Anglo-Saxon, Norman and Latin linguistic heritage, with over 200,000 new trademarks being registered each year, the well of coinable words is fast being drained.

2. Marks That Suggest, But Don't Describe

In general, marketing folks favor suggestive names because they evoke an image or idea that customers are likely to associate with the product or service being marketed. A name is usually considered suggestive when you need to take at least one more mental step to figure out what is being suggested. Here are some examples:

- ask.com, the domain name for the Ask Jeeves search engine, effective because it suggests answers, just what you want a search engine to do
- peapods.com, the domain name for the Pea Pods baby things site, suggests maternity things
- peapod.com, a website featuring online grocery ordering
- Salon.com, an online magazine, suggests a place for the exchange of sophisticated commentary
- eHow.com, a site offering a wide variety of "how to" information
- Travelocity.com, a travel services website, suggests travel and speed
- nextMonet.com, an online contemporary art gallery that suggests undiscovered great artists

- Gazoontite.com (for allergy information and supplies) that suggests the ritualistic and widespread use of the German "Gesundheit!" (health) when someone sneezes
- Getsmart.com, a debt consolidation and loan service, suggests the quality of savvy, something that folks who have debt problems may aspire to, and
- wingspanbank.com (a national online bank) suggests a far-flung presence, something innovative in the banking industry.

Although suggestive names may require some marketing to become broadly identified with a product, they are usually easier to promote than coined names because they already connote something you want to associate with your product or service. Some name consultants argue that suggestive names are the most useful because the images they evoke make them very effective marketing tools. But it may take lots of thought to come up with one that's appropriately evocative, suits your customer base and hasn't been taken. Again, test your ideas out on a number of people to see if they get the message you hope to send.

3. Arbitrary Marks

Words that are descriptive or ordinary when associated with one product or service can be very strong for another. For example, Apple.com is distinctive and legally strong as a trademark because apples have nothing to do with computers, but Swingsets.com for a site that sells children's play equipment is weak because it literally describes the product.

Arbitrary names are fun to invent because you can use any term, or combination of terms, that do not in fact describe your service or product in any way. The trick is to think of a term that is interesting, memorable and somehow appropriate, without literally describing some aspect of your service or product. For example, Yahoo.com is an arbitrary name that would be easy to protect as a trademark.

Clearly, consumer responses to these types of names are subjective and intuitive. If you create an arbitrary mark, try to consider all the possible evocations that the name may have—and make the most of them.

4. Common Terms in Uncommon Arrangements

Ordinary words, in unusual arrangements, can make distinctive names. For example, Magicaldesk.com has weak components—magical and desk are both common terms, but combine them for secretarial services, and the entire name becomes more distinctive and therefore more easily protected.

When evaluating a phrase to see whether it's a strong or weak trademark, it is the overall impression that counts. The fact that some of the elements are ordinary won't matter if the phrase as a whole has an original ring to it. For example, Speedy Turtle Delivery Service is both new and memorable for the contrast of speed and turtle. This makes it distinctive, despite the fact that Speedy Delivery Service without the Turtle would be purely descriptive and so a weak trademark. Especially if you shortened the entire business name to speedyturtle.com, you would have a very distinctive domain name.

USING ONLINE NAME WIZARDS

A number of domain name registrars provide a utility that helps you create possible domain names. For example, NSI's "NameFetcher" asks you to enter three key words that are associated with the name you want. The utility uses a proprietary thesaurus to produce lists of related terms for each of your key words. You are asked to select a term from each list that you might want in your domain name. The utility uses your choices to search the availability of names that contain them.

G. Names to Avoid

There are two categories of names to avoid when selecting your domain name:

- Names that the PTO will refuse to register as trademarks, and
- Names that will be in legal conflict with existing trademarks.

1. Names You Can't Register As Trademarks

If you want to protect your choice of domain name as a trademark, you'll want to register it with the United States Patent and Trademark Office. (Chapter 8 tells you how.) The PTO will not register any of the following:

- Names that contain immoral, deceptive or scandalous matter (essentially, four-letter words)
- Names that disparage or falsely suggest a connection with persons (living or dead), institutions, beliefs or national symbols
- Names identifying a particular living individual (unless his or her consent is obtained) or a deceased president of the United States
- Names that have been taken by an organization that has been granted the exclusive right by statute to use the name, such the Boy Scouts and U.S. Olympic Committee
- Names that are misleading or just plain false, or
- Names that are primarily a geographic name or a surname, unless they have acquired a "secondary meaning," as has, for example, schwab.com.

⚠ **Generic terms used as domain names,** such as coffee.com, will not be entitled to protection as trademarks. See Section C, above, for a discussion of the drawbacks and benefits of generic terms.

2. Names That Will Conflict With Existing Trademarks

You should always keep an eye out for possible legal conflicts when choosing your domain name. Even if you already have a business and have taken the necessary steps to register your name with the county clerk (for sole proprietorships and partnerships) or Secretary of State (for corporations or limited liability companies), you may violate someone's trademark by making your business name your domain name. Thousands of business owners have been stunned to discover that they can't use their chosen business name without running afoul of another business's trademark rights.

As a general rule, avoid domain names that are:

- Close to an existing domain name that is both distinctive and used on a competing website.
- The same as or very similar to a famous commercial name used online (Amazon) or off (McDonald's, Disney). Truly famous names get special protection even if use by someone else wouldn't confuse customers. Under laws known as "dilution" statutes, courts can stop any use of a famous name that is intended to trade off the strength of the name, or that has the effect of tarnishing the trademark's reputation for quality.
- The same as or confusingly similar to the name of a famous living person such as Michael Jordan, Julia Roberts or Hillary Clinton.

In addition, if all of the following four statements are true, you run at least some risk that you'll end up on the wrong end of a dispute over your domain name:

- Another business is already using your proposed domain name, or a term very similar as its trademark

- The other business's mark is distinctive, even if marginally

- The other business started using the mark in actual commerce before you started using your proposed domain name, and

- Either the proposed domain name itself, or the products or services to be sold on your website, would create a likelihood of customer confusion. ■

What to Do If Your Domain Name Is Already Taken

Has the domain name you want already been grabbed by another business? Don't worry; you have options.

A. Use .net or .org

If you are like most businesses, you want .com at the end of your domain name. However, many .com names are unavailable, although the same choices may be available with .net or .org.

The availability of .net or .org is probably small consolation to you. E-commerce businesses often refuse to settle for .net or .org because .com has become, as it was intended to, uniquely associated with commercial activity. If you are one of these .com holdouts, you'll just need to keep plugging away with proposed names until a .com version is available.

If, however, your intended activity involves fostering access to the Internet (perhaps as an Internet service provider) or building a real or virtual organization of some type (as a nonprofit organization, for example), .net or .org may be just fine. In some cases, it may even be beneficial. Take the nonprofit national public radio and television entity, the Public Broadcasting Service (PBS). PBS, which derives its credibility and reputation for independent programming and news reporting from its nonprofit status, chose www.pbs.org for its domain name. By staying away from .com, PBS sent the message that the content on its website is non-commercial, which is appealing to those who support it.

⚠️ Using .net or .org doesn't necessarily shield you from claims of trademark infringement. For instance, Amazon.com recently sued Amazon.gr (.gr is for Greece) for trademark infringement. However, a federal court has ruled that a domain name that ends with .net conveys a non-commercial purpose, which may reduce the likelihood of customer confusion between a .net site and a .com site. (If you want to read the judge's decision, you can find that case, *Avery-Dennison v. Sumpton*, 189 F.3d 868 (9th Cir. 1999). See Section D, below for more on federal trademark infringement and ICANN's dispute resolution policy, which could require you to give up your domain name even if it technically doesn't infringe an existing trademark.)

NEW CHOICES FOR TLDS

According to an announcement by ICANN, the following new TLDs will be available for use sometime in 2001:

- .aero, for air-transport industry sites
- .biz, for business sites
- .coop, for non-profit cooperatives' sites
- .info, for unrestricted use
- .museum, for museums' sites
- .name, for individuals' sites
- .pro, for accountants', lawyers' and physicians' sites.

To find out more about these new TLDs, visit http://www.icann.org/tlds and click on the contact links on the right side of the table. Be sure to check the FAQs on this page before you act. You'll find, for instance, that ICANN discourages pre-registration.

B. Change the Name Slightly

A domain name is reported as not available only if the *exact* name is already taken. For instance, if an availability search tells you that madprophet.com is already taken, you may find that "mad-prophet.com" or "madprophets.com" is available. So, if you are not wed to the exact form of your first proposed domain name, you can experiment with minor variations until you find an acceptable name that is available.

The fact that a slightly different name is available for registration doesn't mean that you can or should use it, however. Using a domain name very similar to an existing one may result in trademark infringement—the violation of someone's trademark rights. If you're found to have infringed someone's trademark, a court could order you to stop using the name and pay money damages to the other domain name owner. The result would depend on whether:

- the name is actually being used on a commercial website, or
- the close similarity in names would be likely to confuse potential customers.

For example, a potential customer who sets out to access the original madprophet site but who mistakenly types in a dash will end up at your site. This may be a temporary diversion, or it may represent the loss of the other site's customer to you. Especially if you are offering competing goods or services, you will have created the exact type of customer confusion that the trademark laws have been designed to protect against.

If you're thinking about choosing a domain name that is only a slight alteration of another site's domain name, read Chapter 7 on customer confusion first.

BAD-FAITH MISSPELLINGS OF EXISTING DOMAIN NAMES

The ICANN arbitration procedure for resolving domain name disputes can result in the loss of your right to use your domain name if an existing trademark/domain name owner shows that you are using the same or confusingly similar mark—in bad faith—as your domain name. For instance, in an arbitration brought by the search engine AltaVista under the ICANN dispute resolution rules, the arbitrator found that domain names such as Actavista.com, Aliavista.com, Autavista.com and Antavista.com had been registered by another company in bad faith and ordered the company to stop using them. A similar arbitration ruling in a different proceeding was made regarding 40 variations of Yahoo. (See Section D2, below, for more information.)

C. Buy the Name

Domain names are bought, sold and auctioned like any other property. If the domain name you want is being used on an actively maintained commercial website, chances are slim the owner will sell it to you. However, if the name has been reserved but isn't being used, you may be able to get it for a price you can afford.

How much is a domain name worth? Most domain names don't sell for that much (though some exceptions are listed in "Big Sellers," below). At GreatDomains.com, the leading online domain name brokerage house, the average offer price is around $32,000, and the average selling price is $14,500.

That website provides an interesting discussion of how it ranks and appraises the value of the domain names it deals in. For a detailed discussion of how this particular brokerage appraises domain names, visit its website at www.GreatDomains.com. The most important factors are:

- the number of characters (the shorter the better)
- the market potential of the business to which the domain name is attached (for example, car.com is more valuable than camping.com because it reaches a broader market); and
- the use of .com, which is better than .net or .org for a commercial enterprise.

You can buy a domain name in a variety of ways. You can look in online classifieds, contact the owner directly and make an offer, make a bid on an auction website (ebay.com, for example) or go through an online domain name broker such as GreatDomains.com.

BIG SELLERS

Prices of some recent big-money transfers of domain names:

business.com	$7.5 million
altavista.com	$3.3 million
wallstreet.com	$1.03 million
computer.com	$500,000
question.com	$175,000
internet.com	$100,000
drugs.com	$823,000
ForSaleByOwner.com	$835,000

If you are buying or selling a domain name through an online broker (like GreatDomains.com), the broker will likely supply all the necessary paperwork to legally transfer the domain name. If you don't use a broker, you or the other party to the deal must supply the purchase agreement. If it falls on you to come up with an agreement, consider adapting the sample agreement below.

SAMPLE DOMAIN NAME TRANSFER AGREEMENT

Domain Name Transfer Agreement

_____ (Buyer)

and _____ (Seller)

agree as follows:

1. Seller assigns to Buyer all right, title and interest worldwide to the _____*[Domain Name]*_____ domain name, together with any goodwill associated with it.

2. Seller represents that Seller has full power to enter into and perform this Agreement.

3. Seller will promptly apply to _*[name of registrar from which Seller purchased the name]*_ to transfer ownership and management of _____*[Domain Name]*_____ to Buyer under current NSI procedures for modifying a domain record. Specifically, Seller will instruct _*[registrar]*_ to change the billing name, technical contact and administrative contact for _____*[Domain Name]*_____ to _*[new billing name, technical contact and administrative contact information]*_. Seller will provide the information and email messages, and execute documents, necessary to accomplish the transfer of the domain name.

4. Buyer will pay Seller $_____ upon confirmation that _____*[registrar]*_____ has changed the billing name, technical contact, and administrative contact as

SAMPLE DOMAIN NAME TRANSFER AGREEMENT (CONTINUED)

specified in Paragraph 2. A current printout of a WHOIS query provided to Buyer by Seller will be sufficient evidence of the domain name transfer. Buyer will issue a check for the full amount made out to _____, and send it via overnight delivery service to Seller at the address below.

5. As a courtesy, Buyer will attempt to forward to Seller from time to time any misdirected email messages received through the _____*[Domain Name]*_____ domain name. Seller recognizes that Buyer's hardware and the Internet itself may not always function perfectly, and that delays might be involved in forwarding the email messages. In no event will Buyer be liable for any lost profits, lost revenue, lost data or any form of special, incidental, indirect, consequential or punitive damages of any kind, whether based on breach of contract or warranty, tort (including negligence), product liability or otherwise (whether or not foreseeable), even if informed in advance of the possibility of such damages, for failure to deliver or timely deliver any email message.

6. This Agreement will be governed by the laws of the State of _____*[Buyer's state]*_____.

7. If any provision of this Agreement is held by a tribunal of competent jurisdiction to be contrary to law, the remaining provisions will remain in effect.

SAMPLE DOMAIN NAME TRANSFER AGREEMENT (CONTINUED)

8. This Agreement constitutes the entire agreement between the parties with respect to the _____*[Domain Name]*_____ domain name. This Agreement may not be changed in any respect except in writing duly executed by authorized representatives of each of the parties.

_____	_____
Seller's Full Name	Buyer's Full Name
_____	_____
Seller's Signature	Buyer's Signature
_____	_____
Date	Date
_____	_____
Address	Address
_____	_____

If you use an online broker, here's how your transaction might work. First, you go to the broker's website. If you find a domain name you want, you submit an offer to the broker, who forwards your offer to the seller. The broker then informs you whether your offer has been accepted, rejected or there is a counteroffer. If your offer has been accepted, the broker mails you a purchase contract and detailed escrow instructions to sign. You pay no broker fees. The seller pays all the fees.

BEWARE OF CYBERSQUATTERS

If the domain name registrant appears eager to sell the name to you and the name is the same or similar to a mark you're already using, take a moment to reflect. It's now illegal, under federal law, to traffic in domain names in this manner. See Section D for a more detailed description of how the law works.

D. Assert Your Rights As Senior Trademark User

 Read the rest of this chapter only if you:
- are already in business
- use a distinctive name to identify your product or service, and
- want to use that name as your domain name.

If you already use your proposed domain name to market products or services, you may have the upper hand in a dispute with someone who's using the domain name. Under trademark law, the first person to use a mark in commerce is considered the owner (more on this in Chapter 3, Section B). So if you used the name to market your products or services before the domain name registrant started using its domain name, you can prevent the use of that name if:

- your mark is nationally famous (laws against trademark dilution protect famous marks from use by others, even if there is no customer confusion—see Chapter 4, Section G2), *or*

- the use of that name creates a likelihood of customer confusion between that business and yours (discussed in some detail in Chapter 7), *or*

- the domain name registrant is a "cybersquatter" under federal law, *or*

- the other user is deemed a bad-faith registrant under the dispute resolution policy.

1. Choosing a Strategy

If you are a trademark holder and want to challenge the use of a domain name, you will first need to decide on a strategy for going after the registrant. You have three choices:

- **Use the dispute resolution service offered by ICANN.** ICANN, the international nonprofit organization now in charge of domain name registrations worldwide, manages a process called the Uniform Domain Name Dispute Resolution Policy, or UDRP. This administrative procedure works only for cybersquatting disputes—that is, when someone has registered your name in a bad-faith attempt to profit from your trademark. It is potentially less expensive (about $750 to $2,500 in fees) and quicker than a lawsuit (just 57 days to resolution).

- **File a trademark infringement lawsuit.** If you win, the court will order the domain name holder to transfer the domain name to you, and may award you money damages as well. A lawsuit is always an option, whether or not you pursue ICANN's dispute resolution process. We discuss infringement lawsuits in Section 3, below.

STRATEGIES FOR GOING AFTER SOMEONE USING YOUR TRADEMARK AS A DOMAIN NAME

	ICANN Dispute Resolution Procedure	Trademark Infringement Lawsuit	Cybersquatting Lawsuit
Lawyer needed?	No	Yes	Yes
Cost	Approximately $750 to $2,500	$10,000 and up	$10,000 and up
Time	57 days from date you file your complaint	Months if the case settles, years if it goes to trial	A month or two
Who can be challenged	Any domain name registrant	As a practical matter, only U.S. registrants	As a practical matter, only U.S. registrants
What you may win	The domain name you want	The domain name you want plus money damages	The domain name you want, plus money damages for post-November 1999 activity

ELEMENTS YOU MUST PROVE IN THE DIFFERENT TYPES OF ACTIONS

ICANN Dispute Resolution Procedure	Trademark Infringement Lawsuit	Cybersquatting Lawsuit Under ACCPA
1. The domain name is identical or confusingly similar to your mark	1. You are the owner of a legitimate trademark (i.e. the mark is distinctive or has acquired secondary meaning)	1. Your mark was distinctive when the domain name was registered
2. The name was registered and used in bad faith, *and*	2. Your mark was used commercially before the domain name was registered, *and*	2. The domain name is identical or confusingly similar to mark
3. The registrant lacks a legitimate interest in name.	3. The registrant's use of the domain name creates a likelihood of customer confusion in the source of the two products.	3. The registrant's acts demonstrate bad faith, *and*
		4. The mark is entitled to protection under federal law.

- **File a cybersquatting lawsuit.** In this case, you will file a lawsuit in federal court arguing that the domain name registrant is in violation of the Anti-Cybersquatting Consumer Protection Act. If you win, you can not only get the domain name you want, you may also win money damages from the cybersquatter.

For more on bad faith, see Section D4, below, which discusses bad faith in the context of a cybersquatting lawsuit. The Anticybersquatting statute lists several indicators of bad faith. Although you could not cite the statute in an ICANN arbitration, you might find that these indicators will help you determine whether you can prove bad faith in the context of an ICANN arbitration.

2. The ICANN Dispute Resolution Procedure

ICANN's dispute resolution procedure applies to virtually all domain name registrants.

CURRENT INFORMATION ABOUT DISPUTE RESOLUTION PROCEDURES

ICANN: http://www.icann.org. Go there for the most current information about the new dispute resolution process.

DomainMagistrate.com: http://www.DomainMagistrate.com. This site is operated by Network Solutions, Inc., to help the public understand the new domain name dispute resolution procedures.

Dispute Resolution Providers: ICANN has named four organizations as official domain name dispute resolution providers:

- The World Intellectual Property Organization (WIPO): http://arbiter.wipo.int/domains
- The National Arbitration Forum: http://www.arbforum.com/domains
- CPR Institute for Dispute Resolution: http://www.cpradr.org, and
- eResolution: http://www.eresolution.ca.

a. What You Must Prove to Win

To win your case in the ICANN procedure, you'll have to prove three things:

- The domain name at issue is identical or confusingly similar to a mark that you own, whether or not the mark has been registered as a trademark in the U.S. or abroad
- The registrant has no rights or legitimate interests in the domain name, and
- The domain name was registered and/or is being used in bad faith.

You must prove similar things to prevail in a lawsuit based on the federal Anti-Cybersquatting Consumer Protection Act, discussed in Section 4, below. As a practical matter, the Anti-Cybersquatting Act is enforceable only in the United States. The ICANN procedure, on the other hand, can conveniently be used against domain name registrants outside of the U.S. as well.

Here's a look at each of these three elements in more detail.

Domain name's confusing similarity to your trademark. You must assert that you own the mark because you were the first to use it or because trademark registration has given you the right to its exclusive use. You must also state that the domain name really is confusingly similar to your mark. (If you need help understanding customer confusion, see Chapter 7.) If the domain name at issue is preventing you from using your mark as your own domain name, the "identical or confusingly similar" test will probably be satisfied.

Registrant's lack of rights or legitimate interests in the name. To prove this element, you must show three things:

- The registrant has never tried to use the domain name (or a similar one) in connection with legitimate commerce, online or off
- The registrant was never generally known by the domain name, even if the name wasn't used in commerce as a trademark, and

- The registrant isn't using the domain name in any legitimate way. A legitimate use would, for example, consist of use on a non-commercial website that engages in satire or criticism. But the use would not be legitimate if the registrant's actual intent is to divert consumers from your website or business location, or to tarnish your mark by lessening its reputation for quality.

Registrant's bad faith. This one is really the flip side of the second item. The registrant has acted in bad faith if you can show any of the following:

- The registrant acquired the domain name with the intent to sell it back to you or your business in particular, or to a competitor of yours, for profit. This wouldn't apply to those who acquire domain names with the intent to auction them off to the highest bidder later, because the plan was not directed specifically at you.

- The registrant has a pattern of acquiring domain names with the intent to block their use by legitimate trademark owners. That is, the registrant is a true cybersquatter. (See Section 4, below.)

- The registrant is a competitor who acquired the domain name primarily to disrupt your business.

- The registrant is using the domain name to attract users to the website by creating customer confusion. (See Chapter 7.)

The list of bad faith factors set out in the ICANN policy is meant to be illustrative, which means an ICANN arbitrator may find bad faith even when none of these particular factors are present. Therefore, you should think broadly when considering whether the registrant acted in bad faith. As an additional guide, we suggest you also study the bad faith factors established by Congress in the ACCPA, the anti-cybersquatting statute. (See Section 4, below.) For instance, one of the possible bad faith factors in a cybersquatting case is that the registrant provided false or misleading contact information to the domain name registry or failed to keep the information up to date. Although this factor is not specifically listed in the ICANN policy, there is no reason why it can't be used to demonstrate bad faith in an ICANN arbitration.

WHY STING LOST AND MADONNA WON

Gordon Sumner, better known as Sting (the entertainer), sought to acquire the domain name sting.com through the ICANN dispute resolution procedure. One of the elements Sting had to prove was that he had trademark rights in the name. Because sting is a commonly used term, the arbitrator decided that there were no such trademark rights and refused to order the registrant to transfer the name.

Madonna obtained a different result when she sought to capture madonna.com from the then current registrant, who was using the name to lead users to a sex site. The registrant had raised the Sting case as a defense, arguing that since madonna, like sting, is a word in the English language, it shouldn't be considered to have trademark status.

This argument was shot down by the arbitrator who pointed out that, while there were many possible reasons to use the word madonna as a domain name, the registrant had failed to state any legitimate reason why he would use the word to lead to a sex site other than to trade on the reputation of the popstar in this area of commerce. In the arbitrator's words, "[W]here no plausible explanation has been provided for adopting a domain name that corresponds to the name of a famous entertainer, other Panels have found a violation of the Policy." Thus, the registrant's intent trumped the trademark status of the term.

Even though the registrant that Madonna filed against was not the original registrant of the address—he had acquired the madonna.com name from an earlier registrant—the arbitrator ruled that acquisition in bad faith was the same as registration in bad faith.

b. How the Process Works

Your first step is to choose a dispute resolution "provider," which is an organization approved by ICANN. So far, ICANN has approved four providers. Each has its own supplemental rules for dispute resolution, so in addition to ICANN's procedural rules you must follow the provider's rules. You can check them out at the provider's website, listed below. These sites offer detailed discussions about how to navigate the process.

To begin your case, you send a complaint to the provider, setting out specific facts that prove the three elements discussed above. Check the provider's website for fee information. Who pays the fees and the amount of fees will vary depending on the circumstances and the provider.

After reviewing the complaint for completeness, the provider will send the registrant a copy of the complaint, along with directions on how the registrant can respond and within how much time. The domain name registrant can continue to use the name until the dispute is resolved.

The provider will usually issue a response based solely on the complaint and the response. Either party may go to court if the decision is not to their liking. However, if the decision is in your favor, you will get the domain name transferred to you unless the registrant promptly files a lawsuit to prevent it.

The ICANN procedure has proved to be a popular way to resolve domain name disputes. Since the procedure's inception in early 2000 (and as of January 21, 2001) 2,715 disputes involving 4,855 domain names have been submitted for resolution. Of the 1,885 proceedings that have been resolved by an arbitration decision, roughly 75% have gone in favor of the trademark owner seeking to cancel a domain name. For more specific and current numbers, visit the ICANN statistical site at http://www.icann.org. Click through to the statistical summary and information from the Domain Name Dispute Resolution (UDRP) page.

The ICANN site posts all arbitration decisions by domain name, date and proceeding number, also available from the UDRP page. It provides a full-text search tool for decisions and for the dispute proceedings index. By spending a little time browsing through the decisions, you will get an excellent idea of how domain name disputes are being handled. Most of the decisions are relatively short and follow a similar format consisting of a brief recitation of the dispute's factual history (who did what and when) and an application of the ICANN criteria for deciding domain name disputes.

c. New Law Emerges From ICANN Arbitrations

Because all UDRP arbitration decisions are stored in an ICANN database (as well as on the websites of the parent dispute resolution providers), arbitrators naturally use this database as guidance when reaching a decision in a similar case. In this sense, a new body of domain name law is being developed in much the same way as the English courts originally developed what we now refer to as the common law.

While the body of arbitration decisions uses the UDRP policies as their starting place, issues raised by the parties sometimes require solutions that aren't addressed in those policies. For instance, arbitrators have used existing legal principles to decide that:

- Once a complainant alleges that the registrant "has no rights or legitimate interests in respect of the domain name," the burden shifts to the registrant to prove that he or she does have such rights or legitimate interests in the name (*Do The Hustle, LLC v. Tropic Web*, WIPO Case No. D2000-0624).

- The registrant's failure to answer written allegations of bad faith sent to the registrant by the complainant was an "admission by silence" that could support the arbitrator's finding of bad faith. (*Cigna Corp. v. JIT Consulting*, eResolution Case No. AF 00174).

- A claimant who failed to prove his case could mount another challenge if new evidence was later discovered. (*Nintendo of America Inc. v. Alex Jones*, WIPO Case No. D2000-0998).

If you are involved in a UDRP proceeding, you can use the ICANN search engine to ferret out previous decisions that may have a bearing on your issues.

USING "SUCKS" WITH A FAMOUS MARK

Many domain names combine the pejorative term "sucks" with a well-known mark (for instance, walmartsucks.com and lucentsucks.com), for the purpose of indicating that the site contains matter critical of the company that owns the mark. Companies subjected to the suck treatment have understandably been upset and sought injunctive relief in the federal courts under trademark infringement and dilution laws. For the most part, these efforts to squash suck sites have failed for two reasons: 1) trademark infringement usually depends on a finding of likely customer confusion, and there is little possibility that potential customers would think that the suck site is sponsored by the original mark's owner, and 2) even when confusion is not an issue, as in dilution cases, the courts have applied the First Amendment to permit the use of suck with a famous mark to lead to sites that really do contain comment on and criticism of the original mark's owner.

UDRP arbitrators have been careful to look for the true intent of "suck" sites. Arbitrators have found that: (1) Suck names should be considered confusingly similar to the original mark when the registrant intended to simply harass the mark's owner or cause the owner to buy the name back, rather than truly establish a legitimate complaint and commentary site, and (2) the bad faith implicit in registering a domain name containing a legitimate mark for commercial or harassment purposes exempts the name from First Amendment protection and supports a decision requiring the registrant to transfer the suck name to the original mark's owner.

The key lesson to be learned from these UDRP cases is that if you want to use a suck domain name, make sure the website to which it leads is non-commercial and is registered purely for the purpose of criticism and comment. See, for example, *Diageo plc v. John Zuccarini, Individually and t/a Cupcake Patrol*, WIPO Case No. D2000–0996 (involving the name Guinesssucks) and *Wal-Mart Stores, Inc. v. Walsucks and Walmarket Puerto Rico*, WIPO Case No. D2000-0477.

3. A Trademark Infringement Lawsuit

As the senior user of a trademark, you can bring a trademark infringement lawsuit against the domain name owner if the use of the domain name creates a likelihood of customer confusion with your valid trademark. As part of this suit, you can ask the court to require the owner of the domain name to transfer it to you, and you may also be able to recover damages and attorney's fees. Of course, going to court is time-consuming and may cost you more than you'll recover from the defendant. You'll want to carefully weigh the possible benefits against the costs.

Things can get confusing if the trademark you've been using isn't exactly the same as your proposed domain name. If it's almost the same, trademark law lets you maintain ownership. But you can lose your seniority if there are *significant* differences. For instance, in one recent case, a company that owned the trademark "The Movie Buff's Movie Store" registered the domain name moviebuff.com. Another company, which had been using the actual mark "moviebuff" on a CD-ROM containing movie information, wanted the moviebuff.com domain name. The "Movie Buff's Movie Store" mark was used before the other company started using moviebuff on its CD-ROMs. Who was the senior user of the moviebuff trademark? A federal appeals court ruled that "The Movie Buff's Movie Store" was an entirely different mark than moviebuff, and ordered the "Movie Buff's Movie Store" company to surrender the domain name to the moviebuff company. (*Brookfield v. West Coast Entertainment Corp.*, 174 F.3d 1036 (9th Cir. 1999).

Trademark: Legal Care for Your Business & Product Name, by Stephen Elias (Nolo), is a book that explains how rights to conflicting trademarks are resolved and what's typically involved in trademark infringement actions

Trademark Disputes: Who Wins, Who Loses & Why, by Stephen Elias, is a downloadable eGuide, available at http://www.nolo.com.

4. An Anti-Cybersquatting Lawsuit

If you own a trademark and find that someone or some business is holding it hostage as a domain name until you pay a large sum for it, you may be the victim of cybersquatting. You can sue to get your domain name—and possibly some money damages—under a 1999 federal law known as the Anti-Cybersquatting Consumer Protection Act. Because suits must be filed in federal court, you almost certainly will need to hire a lawyer.

Under the Act, cybersquatting means registering, trafficking in or using a domain name with bad-faith intent to profit from the goodwill of a mark belonging to someone else. It refers to the practice of buying up domain names reflecting the names of existing businesses with the intent of selling the names for a profit back to the businesses when they want to set up websites.

THE ORIGINS OF CYBERSQUATTING

The practice that's come to be known as cybersquatting originated at a time when most businesses were not savvy about the commercial opportunities on the Internet. Some entrepreneurial souls registered the names of well-known companies as domain names, with the intent of selling the names back to the companies when they finally woke up. Panasonic, Fry's Electronics, Hertz and Avon were among the "victims" of cybersquatters. Opportunities for cybersquatters are rapidly diminishing, because most businesses now know that nailing down domain names is a high priority and that cybersquatting is an actionable offense.

a. Recognizing Cybersquatting

How do you know if a cybersquatter has your name? As a general rule, you should first see whether your proposed but unavailable domain name belongs to a legitimate website. Enter the address into your browser and see what you find.

If the domain name takes you to a website that appears to be functional and reasonably related in its subject matter to the domain name, you probably aren't facing a case of cybersquatting. However, you may have a case of trademark infringement, as described in Section 3, above.

If your browser produces any of the following results, and you are a famous individual or are using your existing business name as your proposed domain name, you may have a case of cybersquatting on your hands:

- You get a "can't find server" message
- You get an "under construction" page, or
- You get a page that appears to have no relationship to the meaning of the domain name.

Although each of these results suggests the possibility of cyber-squatting, there may be an innocent explanation for the lack of a functioning or relevant website, especially if the website is still under construction. It's very easy and inexpensive to register or reserve domain names but more difficult to put up the actual website. You can reserve a domain name for up to ten years, so the fact that a website is not up, even months after the name was reserved or registered, does not necessarily mean that the registrant doesn't have perfectly legitimate plans to have a website in the future.

Before jumping to any conclusions about an unavailable domain name, contact the registrant with information you find at http://www.whois.net. (See Chapter 2, Section B, for a refresher on "who is.") Find out whether there is a reasonable explanation for the use of the name, or if the registrant is willing to sell you the name at a price you are willing to pay.

Sometimes paying the cybersquatter is the best choice. Even though Congress has provided a remedy against cybersquatting, it requires a federal court lawsuit and, almost by necessity, lawyers. It may be a lot cheaper and quicker for you to come to terms with a cybersquatter than to stand on your rights and invoke the power of the federal court with its attendant costs and delay. Although you may be able to recover your costs and attorney fees if you win, there is no guarantee; it's completely up to the judge.

If a cybersquatting suit does not seem economically feasible, remember that the ICANN dispute resolution policy discussed in Section D2 above may get you what you want for a much cheaper price.

b. What You Must Prove to Win

To win a federal cybersquatting lawsuit, you'll have to prove all of the following:

- The registrant had a bad-faith intent to profit from your mark (see Section c, below)
- Your mark was distinctive at the time the domain name was first registered, in that it was either inherently distinctive or had become distinctive by acquiring secondary meaning (see Chapter 4 for more on what makes a mark distinctive)
- The domain name is identical or confusingly similar to your mark, and
- Your mark qualifies for protection under federal trademark laws (see Chapter 8)—that is, you were the first to use the mark in commerce.

You don't have to show that customers are likely to be confused. (This is different from a trademark infringement lawsuit; see Section 2 above.) This means you can sue the domain name registrant even if the website sells products or services that are completely unrelated to yours.

c. Bad Faith

To win a lawsuit based on the Anti-Cybersquatting Act, you must show bad faith on the part of the domain name registrant. In Section 2, above, we explored the issue of bad faith as measured by the factors in the ICANN dispute resolution policy. In this section, we discuss bad faith in terms of the factors in the anti-cybersquatting statute. The two sets of bad faith factors are different but complementary—they both point to acts by the registrant that indicate an intent to use the domain name to profit at the expense of a specific trademark owner.

Importantly, both lists of bad faith factors are intended to be illustrative rather than exhaustive, which means that ICANN arbitrators (who will be guided by ICANN's policies) and federal court judges (who will follow the Anti-Cybersquatting Act) may find the existence of bad faith even if none of the listed factors are present. In other words, do not feel limited by either set. If you want to know whether the domain name registrant in your dispute was guilty of bad faith that will support a judgment in an anti-cybersquatting lawsuit, you should study the bad faith factors in our discussion of ICANN's procedures (see Section 2), in addition to the factors set out in this section. For instance, the ICANN policy lists as a bad faith factor the fact that the registrant "registered the domain name primarily for the purpose of disrupting the business of a competitor." Although this factor isn't explicitly mentioned as a bad faith factor in the anti-cybersquatting statute, it would almost certainly be considered as proof of bad faith by a federal court.

The factors listed in the anti-cybersquatting statute as indicators of the bad faith necessary to prove a cybersquatting are:

- **Is the registrant using the domain name to divert users from your site to a site where customer confusion is likely to result or your trademark's reputation for quality is harmed?** In other words, is the domain name being used in a way that negatively affects your website or the value of your trademark?

- **Has the registrant offered to sell the domain name to you without having ever legitimately used the domain name on a commercial website?**

- **Has the registrant provided false or misleading contact information to the domain name registry or failed to keep this information up to date?**

- **Has the registrant registered multiple names that are the same or confusingly similar to distinctive marks?** In other words, is there an apparent pattern of cybersquatting?

- **Is the mark in question famous or highly distinctive?** The more distinctive or famous the mark, the more the court is likely to conclude that the registrant acted in bad faith.

If the answer to any of these questions is yes, the court may be inclined to find that the registrant is acting in bad faith, or did so when the domain name was registered. For example, in January 2001, Volkswagen succeeded in using the anticybersquatting statute to win the address vw.net from its registrant. The Fourth Circuit Court of Appeals found bad faith where the registrant had originally registered the name hoping to sell it later to Volkswagen "for a lot of money" and had never used the famous mark "VW" for a legitimate business. (*Virtual Works, Inc. v. Volkswagen of America, Inc.*, No. 00-1356 (4th Cir. Jan. 22, 2001).) Again, a court may be influenced by other types of behavior, such as those listed in the ICANN procedures, above.

Despite the large number of possible activities that might indicate bad faith in a cybersquatting case, none of them will matter if there is sufficient evidence that the registrant's use or registration of the domain name was a fair use or otherwise lawful. If a domain name registrant is able to come up with a reason for the registration other than to profit from it in some way at the trademark owner's expense (such as selling it back to the trademark owner or diverting traffic from the trademark owner's website on the basis of customer confusion), then the court will most likely side with the registrant.

If you can answer yes to any of the following questions, then there is a likelihood that no bad faith will be found:

- **Does the domain name registrant have an arguable claim to the name because of the registrant's existing trademark rights?** There may be concurring uses of the same name that are noninfringing, such as the use of the "Delta" trademark for both air travel and sink faucets. Similarly, the registration of the domain name "deltaforce.com" by a movie studio would not tend to indicate a bad-faith intent on the part of the registrant to trade on Delta Airlines' or Delta Faucets' trademarks.

- **Does the domain name identify the registrant as an individual?** A person is entitled to his or her own name, whether in business or on a website. Similarly, a person may bear a legitimate nickname that is identical or similar to a well-known trademark, such as in the well-publicized case of the parents who registered the domain name "pokey.org" for their young son who goes by that name.

- **Has the registrant ever used the domain name in connection with the offering of goods or services?** If the registrant has a commercially sensible reason for using the domain name (other than selling it back to you, that is), there is probably not bad faith.

- **Is the registrant legally using the mark on the website itself?** It's legal to make noncommercial or fair uses of others' marks online, such as in comparative advertising, comment, criticism, parody or news reporting. However, the fact that the domain name is used for one of these purposes would not alone establish a lack of bad faith.

IT'S THE FACTS THAT COUNT

In one of the first cases decided under the federal anti-cybersquatting law, a court ruled that a business that had used another business's trademark as a domain name had acted in bad faith and was a cybersquatter.

In 1985, Sportsman's Market (Sportman's) registered the trademark Sporty's, which it used on its aviation products catalog. Ten years later, Omega Engineering decided to sell aviation products and registered the domain name sportys.com. Nine months later, Omega created a wholly-owned subsidiary called "Sporty's Farms" for the alleged purpose of operating a Christmas tree farm, and sold the sportys.com domain name to it. Sportsman's learned of the registration, sued to obtain the domain name for its own use and won in U.S. District Court. Sporty's Farms appealed the trial court's decision.

During the appeal, Congress passed the Anti-Cybersquatting Act, and the appeals court applied it to this dispute. The court noted that the particular facts in this case didn't mesh well with the criteria set out in the Act for determining bad faith, a necessary ingredient for a successful cybersquatting charge. However, the court also noted that the Act allowed it to go beyond those criteria and, under the unique facts of this case, found that Omega had acted in bad faith. Sportsman's got the domain name sportys.com. (*Sporty's Farm v. Sportsman's Market, Inc.,* 202 F.3d 489 (2d Cir. 2000).)

d. What You Can Sue For

Under the Anti-Cybersquatting Act, victorious cybersquatting victims can ask the court for an injunction against the cybersquatter, and for monetary damages.

An injunction is a court order requiring the domain name registrant to transfer the domain name to the plaintiff. Injunctive relief is available whether the cybersquatting occurred before or after the Act took effect.

RECOVERING YOUR GOOD NAME

If a cybersquatter has registered your personal name—or a name that is "substantially or confusingly similar" to it—you can sue in federal court to have the name transferred back to you. However, you will have to prove that the domain name registration was done with the specific intent of selling it back to you or to a third party for a profit. As a general rule, this will only work for famous people and politicians, since it's unlikely that the name would be registered with an intent to make a profit unless it belonged to someone well known.

If you win your lawsuit against the cybersquatter, you are also entitled to recover three times the total amount of money you lost because of the cybersquatter, plus the profits realized by the cybersquatter from his or her illegal activity, plus your court costs. In exceptional cases, you can also be awarded attorney's fees. However, cybersquatting usually doesn't cause actual monetary losses (though it does cause you massive inconvenience). Nor does it generate profits, unless you paid the squatter. So, at your option, the Court can award you "statutory damages" of $1,000 to $100,000. Since statutory damages do not require proof of any type, they offer you a realistic opportunity to recover money as well as the domain name.

Importantly, money damages (both actual and statutory) may only be recovered for cybersquatting activity that occurred after November 29, 1999. For instance, if the cybersquatting activity complained of is the registration of the name, and the registration occurred before November 29, 1999, you can't recover money damages. However, you can recover for other prohibited activities that occurred after November 29, 1999. For example, even if the domain name was registered before November 29, 1999, you can still recover money damages if the domain name was trafficked in (for instance, offered for sale) or used after November 29, 1999.

IF YOU CAN'T FIND THE CYBERSQUATTER

You may run into trouble when you try to sue a cybersquatter, if you don't have a physical address where the cybersquatter can be reached. A lawsuit generally can't begin until the person or business is properly notified that it's being sued. And you can't send that notification (including a complaint and a summons to appear) by email. Some cybersquatters provide inaccurate contact information to the domain name registration service, making them next to impossible to track down.

If you can convince the court that you've been diligent in trying to locate the cybersquatter, but have failed to do so, the court will allow the action to proceed and may order the registration service to give you the name. This is called an "in rem" action.

■

CHAPTER 6

Making Sure Your Domain Name Doesn't Conflict With Another Business's Trademark

If your domain name is the same or very similar to another business's trademark, the trademark owner may someday (maybe someday soon) force you to stop using the name. Only by doing a search can you be reasonably assured that you have a legal right to use your proposed domain name. This chapter explains how to do your own search on the Internet or how to hire and use a trademark search service.

There are actually two elements you need to consider when determining whether or not your domain name may violate someone else's trademark rights. The first question, which you can answer with a trademark search, is whether your domain name is identical or very close to an existing trademark. The second issue is whether or not your use of the domain name would confuse customers or otherwise damage the trademark owner's business or reputation. Deciding whether the simultaneous use of two similar trademarks is likely to create customer confusion is not always easy. (Chapter 7 discusses how to make this assessment; a consultation with a trademark attorney also may be wise, especially in close cases.)

For example, suppose you decide to start an online business auctioning small antique collectibles electronically and at discounted prices. Your location in part of the San Francisco Bay Area called the East Bay prompts you to seek the domain name Ebaybuys.com. You search to see if the domain name is available and you find that it is. You then check the PTO's website, where you conduct a search of the PTO's registered and pending trademarks database using the instructions in Section C, below. You find the name eBay is registered to eBay, Inc., and that eBay, Inc. is using the domain name ebay.com to auction antiques and collectibles as well as other types of goods.

The names eBay and Ebaybuys obviously differ, but they may be close enough to confuse people. Because you also auction antiques, consumers might go to your website when they really wanted to go to eBay's website. Or they might think that you are affiliated with eBay because your domain name also uses the letters "bay" as the root. This potential for consumer confusion means you are probably in danger of infringing eBay, Inc.'s, trademark.

 Be wary of search offers. Lots of banner ads on domain-name related websites offer services, including trademark searches. There is only one comprehensive trademark database available online for free—the one offered by the U.S. Patent and Trademark Office and described in this chapter. Any other type of search is likely to cost you. It may be worth your while to pay for a competent search, but read this chapter before signing up. It may be that the service will charge you for the kind of search you can easily do yourself for free.

A. What Is a Trademark Search?

You need to engage in a systematic hunt for any trademarks that are the same or similar to your domain name. If you find any such trademarks, you'll need to determine (with the help of Chapter 7) whether or not using your domain name would be likely to confuse customers.

There are three main categories of trademarks to search:

- Registered trademarks—trademarks that have been registered with the U.S. Patent and Trademark Office (PTO)
- Pending registration trademarks—names for which applications for registration have been filed with the PTO and are pending further action, and
- Unregistered trademarks—trademarks that are being used in commerce but aren't pending or registered.

B. Should You Do It Yourself?

There are three ways to conduct a trademark search. You can:

- Do it yourself using free online databases
- Hire a search service or an attorney to do it for you, or
- Do some of it yourself and hire someone to do the rest.

The third approach may give you the best legal protection for your time and money. Using your computer to search for registered trademarks on the PTO's website is quick and easy and can provide good preliminary information. But before you put any serious money into building and marketing your own website, it would be wise to put your choice of domain name through a more thorough search for both registered and unregistered marks. You can do this more rigorous search yourself if you are willing to climb a moderate learning curve. (See Section D, below.) Or, you can hire a trademark search service to do it for you. Count on paying roughly $200 to $400 per name. There are some things that a search service can do more efficiently (and often more inexpensively) than you can do for yourself. (See Section E, below.)

C. How to Do Your Own Trademark Search Online

Searching for registered or pending trademarks on your own by using the PTO's online trademark database is easy. A typical search takes only about 15 minutes. You can make best use of your time by downloading the PTO's help file and studying it before starting your search.

This search allows you to compare your proposed domain name with registered trademarks and trademarks that are pending registration with the PTO. The results you come up with will include a list of the trademarks that meet your search parameters, and the names, addresses and contact information of the owners of those trademarks. You'll also learn how the trademark is being used (on what products or for what services) and what "international class" (category of goods or services) the mark has been assigned to by the trademark owner or applicant. This information is key in deciding whether you can go ahead and use the name without creating the likelihood of customer confusion. (See Chapter 7 for more on the international trademark classification scheme and why it matters in cases of apparent conflict.)

⚠️ **Before you launch, get an in-depth search.** The step-by-step instructions in this chapter are limited to how to do a free search on the Web for registered and unregistered trademarks likely to conflict with your proposed domain name. For most people this level of search is just fine as a first step, but this chapter doesn't pretend to teach you the many tricks of the trade used by skilled trademark searchers. Before investing a lot of time and money promoting your website under your chosen domain name, you will be wise to conduct a more intensive search or pay a pro to do it for you. (See Sections D and E, below.)

1. Meet TESS—The Trademark Electronic Search System

TESS is an acronym for Trademark Electronic Search System, the PTO's brand-new search system that the public can use for free on the PTO's website. It is about as good a system as you can find anywhere and is roughly equivalent to the PTO's internal trademark search system known as X-Search. It's updated every day, has enormous flexibility in terms of the type of search that may be performed and all in all is a most valuable gift from the federal government. TESS comes with its own comprehensive help file. If you are doing your own trademark search you will be wise to study it before beginning your search.

2. Go to the Trademark Database

The first step is to go to the PTO's website at http://www.uspto.gov. Click the Trademark Electronic Business Center icon and you'll come to a page with several choices. Select the search option and you'll encounter the page set out below as Figure 1.

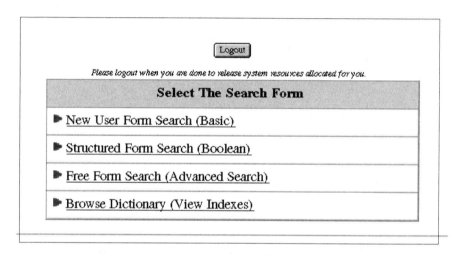

Figure 1

3. Choose the Type of Search

TESS offers four basic approaches to searching:

- New User Form Search
- Structured Form Search
- Free Form Search (Advanced Search), and
- Browse Dictionary.

The New User Form Search is the simplest type of search. It lets you search a limited number of sections of the trademark records, in a limited number of ways. The search has three options for search formats (all the words you list, any of the words you list or the exact phrase you list).

For most searches, the New User Form Search will do just fine. However, as you become more familiar with searching techniques, you'll probably want to use the Structured Form Search or Free Form Search because of their added flexibility. For instance, the Structured Form Search gives you access to all the fields in the trademark record and offers greater search format options. The Free Form Search (advanced search) goes a step further by allowing you to construct searches of unlimited complexity. See Section 8, below, for more on the Free Form Search.

Regardless of which of these three search approaches you decide to use, you'll also want to do a quick browse through the dictionary.

⚠️ **Timed Out by TESS.** In order to maintain its system resources, the TESS program will terminate your searching session after 15 minutes of inactivity. All searches and results will be lost and you will receive a message: "This search session has expired. Please start a search session again by clicking on the TRADEMARK icon, if you wish to continue." You must exit and re-enter TESS to continue searching. To keep from losing your search results, you can save individual searches in an html file by using the "save" feature of your browser.

4.   Browse the Dictionary

The dictionary is an alphabetical listing of all the marks that appear in the TESS database. Suppose that you wish to search for the mark "Domain." You'd click the "Browse Dictionary" link and enter the name "domain" in the search box. After clicking the browse button, you'd see the page set out below as Figure 2.

Term	Docs	Hits
DOMAGIC*	2	2
DOMAGI*	2	2
DOMAGNE	1	1
DOMAG*	3	3
DOMAID	1	1
DOMAIN	2373	4512
DOMAINALYZER	1	4
DOMAINALYZER*	1	1
DOMAINALYZE*	1	1
DOMAINALYZ*	1	1
DOMAINALY*	1	1

[Browse Next Page]   [Browse First Page]

Figure 2

By obtaining a listing of marks that alphabetically precede and follow the name you're searching, you can get a quick overview of marks that are alphabetically close to yours.

Sometimes you will encounter a list of marks in the dictionary that starts with the full word and then shows the same word several times with a decreasing number of letters at the end. For example, browsing for the word "domain" also shows domainalyzer, domainalyzer*, domainalyze*, domainalyz* and domainaly*. The terms with the asterisk in this example are not themselves registered marks but rather are roots of the term domainalyzer. They show up separately on the list because of internal PTO search protocols. In other words, terms with asterisks that follow a term without an asterisk may safely be ignored.

5. Understanding the TESS Structured Form Search

The Structured Form Search is almost as easy as to use as the New User Form Search and offers much greater flexibility in searching. For this reason, we are using the Structured Form Search for our step-by-step explanation. Let's first take a look at the Structured Form Search page (see Figure 3, below).

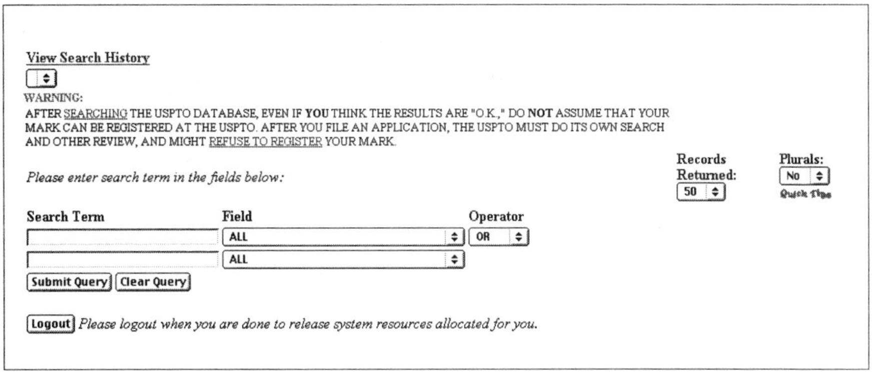

Figure 3

a. Search History

The first active link is titled Search History and is designed to keep track of your searches so you can easily go back over ground that you covered before. Each previous query is identified with a number, as in s1, s2 and so on. You can reproduce the search by simply entering the search number into the first Search Term box. The Search History function operates on all four types of searches offered by TESS. But beware. As we mentioned above, the system will kick you off after 15 minutes of inaction, and when you are kicked off, your Search History is lost. Unfortunately, you cannot save your Search History from one session to another.

b. Records Returned

This drop-down menu gives you the option of returning 50, 100 or 200 records as a result of your search. The default is 50 and there is little reason to change it unless your search results indicated that a larger number of records met your search specifications.

c. Plural

This drop-down menu allows you to retrieve automatically the plural as well as singular forms of words that you enter into the Search Terms box. The default choice is no, but most searchers will want to change this to yes unless they are using the truncation feature. (See Section 6e, below, for more on truncations.)

d. Search Terms

The Structured Form Search lets you search for one or two terms. The terms can be individual words or they can be phrases. You may only need to search for one term. For instance, assume you plan to start a baking company and your first product will be called Mandalay Lemon Pies. You might want to search only for the word "Mandalay," the distinctive element of your name. If so, you would enter that word in the top search box and then click "Submit Query." Or, if you want to see if there are any marks containing the terms "lemon pie," you could enter that exact phrase—surrounded by quotation marks—in the top search box and conduct your search that way. You also may want to find out whether there were any lemon products out there using the term Mandalay. To do this, you could enter "lemon" in the top search box, "mandalay" in the bottom search box and use the pull down "connector" box to indicate that you want to find all marks that contain both terms (discussed just below).

e. Title Field

This drop-down menu lets you specify which specific fields of the TESS database records you want to search. Every trademark record is contained in a number of fields, including the owner of the trademark, the registration date, the registration number, a description of the goods or services that the mark is used to market, the classification assigned to the mark by the Patent and Trademark Office (PTO) and the language of the mark itself. If you only want to search for terms in the marks themselves, then you should choose the Basic Index field. On the other end of the spectrum, if you wish to produce every record that contains your search terms regardless of which field they occur in, select the "all" fields option.

If you are searching for two terms, you can choose separate fields for each term. For instance, you might want to use the Description of Mark field for the term in the top box and the Basic Index field for the term in the lower box.

f. Logical Operators

If you enter terms in both the top and bottom Search Term boxes, you'll need to pick what's called a "Boolean operator" to connect them. You can use the drop-down menu to choose among the available operators.

The AND Operator

If you select AND from the pull-down menu of operators, you are telling TESS to show all trademark records that contain both of the search terms entered in the search term boxes. For example, the search query "shark AND talk" will produce every record that contains both the word "shark" and the word "talk." It will not produce a record that doesn't have both. The advantage of using AND is that you can narrow your search to only those marks that have both terms. The disadvantage to AND is that you won't get any marks that don't have both terms as you have entered them in the Search Term box, which means you might miss marks that you should know about.

The OR Operator

If you enter these same search terms but select the OR operator—making your query "shark OR talk"—your search will produce a list of all trademarks with the term "talk," all trademarks with the term "shark," and all trademarks with both terms. Needless to say, such a list would be very long, because so many trademarks are likely to have either term in them. However, this approach can be useful if your proposed mark contains two distinctive words and you want to review every trademark that has either word. For instance, suppose you're considering the mark AnalogAstromaps for a website featuring a series of star charts. You would most likely want to use the OR operator to search for any trademarks containing either "analog" or "astromaps." Any trademark with either term might knock out your proposed mark if the context showed a likelihood of customer confusion.

Although the OR operator has the advantage of inclusiveness—as compared to the AND operator—it can have the disadvantage of producing much too long a list of marks to intelligently assess. The more common the terms being searched, the greater the risk of an unwieldy number of results. Probably the best approach is to use the OR operator initially and see what turns up. If the results list is too long, you can retreat to the more restrictive AND operator.

The NOT Operator

A third operator—NOT—can be used to exclude from the search results any term you enter in the lower Search Term box. For instance, you may decide that you want to see every trademark with the term "astromap" but no trademark with the term "starchart." This search query would look like this: "astromap NOT starchart."

The XOR Operator

A fourth operator—XOR—lets you search for any trademark that has either the first Search Term or the second Search Term, but not both. For example, if you searched for "analog XOR astromap," your search would turn up trademarks with either "analog" or "astromap," but not trademarks that contain both terms. There is seldom a reason to exclude a combination of two terms

Additional Operators

The TESS Structured Form Search provides additional operators that are most appropriate for searching fields in the trademark records that contain whole sentences or paragraphs. For instance, you can specify that the two terms you enter in the boxes be in the same sentence (WITH) or paragraph (SAME), or within a certain proximity of each other (for instance, within two words of each other in any order (NEAR)), or in the order specified (ADJ). You will find these operators most helpful if you want to search the "Goods and Services" or "Description of Mark" fields. For most trademark searching purposes, however, the AND, OR and NOT operators should be sufficient.

6. Tips on Using the TESS Structured Form Search

As mentioned, TESS provides help for each aspect of the Structured Form Search. However, there is always room for improvement. The tips we outline here are specifically intended for basic trademark searching. As you get more familiar with TESS, you should feel free to experiment with the many options it offers.

a. Focus On the Most Distinctive Part of the Mark

You should focus on the part of your mark that is most distinctive, because it is that part of your mark that would most likely cause customers to confuse your name with an existing trademark using that same term. For instance, if your proposed domain name is zoroasterdesigns.com, the word to use in your search is "zoroaster," since it is by far the more distinctive of the two words. "Designs" is a generic word that can be used in a lot of different trademarks without creating customer confusion. So, although you may wish to search for any mark that contains either "designs" or "zoroaster"—just to see what's out there—you are primarily interested in "zoroaster."

b. Search for Distinctive Syllables

It is wise to go a step further and search for marks that contain one or more of the distinctive syllables in your name. For example, if your proposed mark is Bioscan.com, you should search for trademarks that contain either "bio" or "scan," because you might turn up something similar like "biosearch" or "cellscan." But it wouldn't make much sense to search for marks containing syllables that wouldn't likely be used. For example, the syllables "ga," "zoon" and "tite" (as in the website gazoontite.com) are not nearly as likely to be used in existing marks as are "bio" or "scan."

c. Don't Include ".com" in Your Search

Even though a large number of domain names are being registered as marks, for example, *priceline.com*, it is the portion of the name to the left of the dot that will create the trademark conflict. The PTO requires that the registrant disclaim the ".com" portion of the mark because it is a generic term. This is true for all top level domains, including .org, .net and the new top level domains to be added sometime in 2001. (For more information on registering domain names as trademarks see Chapter 8.)

There are two reasons that you may be searching for conflicts for your proposed domain name. You may be seeking to federally register your domain name or you may be seeking to determine if your proposed domain name (regardless of whether you will federally register it) will conflict with a registered trademark. In either case, when checking for trademark conflicts with domain names, the best approach is to separate the domain name into its various components and search only for the distinctive components.

For instance, in our zoroasterdesigns.com example, you would start your search with "zoroaster." That search would turn up all federally registered zoroaster marks (including those with the .com or any other top level domain name suffix such as .org or .net). This is especially important when choosing a domain name, since the owner of a federally registered mark can stop you from using a similar mark as your domain name if you are offering similar products or services. For example, the owner of the federally registered mark *Zoroaster Furniture* might be able to stop your use of zoroasterdesigns.com if your website offered furniture or similar goods.

d. Searching for Phrases

You can use two or more words as a single search term by enclosing them in quotation marks. For example, a sensible search for "Big Daddy's Sweet Tooth Donuts" would include a search for the phrase "Big Daddy's" and the phrase "Sweet Tooth." You would do this by entering: "Big Daddy" in quotation marks in the upper Search Term box and "Sweet Tooth" in quotation marks in the lower Search Term box.

If you only want to search for a single phrase, such as "Sweet Tooth Munchies," simply enter the phrase in quotation marks in the Search Term box and run the search. You cannot use the truncation feature described in Section e, below, when enclosing a phrase in quotation marks.

e. Use the Truncation Feature Where Appropriate

One of the options offered by TESS is called "word truncation." When you search for a particular term, it's also useful to search for slight variations of the term—for instance, if you are searching for the word "saber," you'll want to know about trademarks using the British spelling, "sabre." The computer won't find these variants for you without special instructions. Fortunately, it's easy to locate slight variations with TESS by using the truncation feature.

Right Truncation

Right truncation allows you to chop off as much of the right-hand portion of a word as you wish and have the computer search for all words that start with what's left. For instance, instead of wondering whether to search for "sabre" or "saber," you could search for all trademarks that begin with the letters "sab." This search would pull up both variations of "saber," but would also produce unrelated terms, such as "sabbath." To create this truncation effect, simply put an asterisk at the end of the string of letters that you want to search, as in "sab*."

If you are using "right truncation," turn off the plural function. You can do this by choosing "No" from the drop down menu above the Operator Box. Otherwise, the search engine will become confused. In addition, you cannot use the truncation feature when enclosing a phrase in quotation marks. For example, the TESS system will not retrieve truncations for the phrase "Big Daddy*" when it is enclosed in quotation marks.

Left Truncation

If you use left truncation, for example on the search "*time," the search results will produce all marks that have letters or words to the left of "time," such as *Drive Time*, *Doubletime* and *Comfy Time*. Unlike right truncation, the plural function works fine with left truncation.

Using Both Left and Right Truncation

TESS allows you to search for words that have both left truncations and right truncations. For instance, if you want to use the word Geezer in your domain name, you might want to do a search for all marks that contain the "eez" portion of the word, since all marks with those three letters will resemble each other at least a little bit. You would get this result by truncating "eez" with an asterisk on both sides. Again, remember to turn off the plural function.

Wildcards

TESS also allows you to substitute "wildcard" characters for specific letters in a word. For instance, if you want to search for all occurrences of women or woman, you should enter the search term wom?n, which would retrieve both words because the question mark stands for any character in that particular position.

TESS comes with an entire set of wildcards, such as characters that stand for vowels, consonants and the like. As you become more familiar with trademark searching in the TESS system, you'll pick these up as you go along.

f. Search for Sound-Alikes

In addition to searching for names that are similar to yours in appearance, it is also important to search for words that sound like your term. For example, gazoontite.com and gesundheit.com don't look that much alike, but they sound identical and might well confuse customers. The best approach to searching for sound-alikes is to focus on the most distinctive syllables in the proposed mark and search for these by themselves. You might pull up a longer list of marks than you want to deal with, but if you do find a mark that sounds like yours and is in use with goods or services that are commercially related to yours, you would do well to choose another mark.

g. Search for Foreign Translations

If your mark has exactly the same meaning as another mark in a different language, the owner of the other mark can challenge your mark if it can be shown that customers would likely be confused. For instance, if you want to name your website milkhouse.com and someone already has a mark for Casa De Leche, you have the potential for a trademark infringement charge. The bad news is that there is no do-it-yourself trademark search system that pulls up translations. The good news is that these types of conflicts are relatively rare. If you are using distinctive terms in your mark that have an independent meaning (which would be the case with arbitrary or suggestive marks), consider using a foreign language dictionary to find translations and then search for those as well as your proposed mark.

7. Trademark Searching With TESS: A Real-Life Example

Bob and Steve have played tennis together for many years. When they hit their mid-fifties, one or the other would occasionally show up with a minor injury (sore shoulder, tender elbow) that dictated a change of pace in the game. They invented some special rules to make the game more easygoing when one of them needed a break. Bob and Steve started to refer to the rules—and the game they produced—as "Geezer Tennis." Aha, a good title for a humorous book. And perhaps the term Geezer Sports might be used on a line of books and other products for aging athletes, which could be sold online at geezersports.com.

Steve checks with Register.com (http://www.register.com) and finds that geezersports.com is available for domain name registration. He then decides to use TESS to do a trademark search, to see whether Geezer Sports is available as a trademark. He enters "Geezer" in the top Search Term box and "Sports" in the lower Search Term box. He turns the plural option on (he's not using right truncation and so the plural option is appropriate), selects AND from the pull-down menu of operators and changes the drop-down menu for fields to "basic index."

The search results show no registered or pending trademark using "Geezer Sports." Now what? Steve takes another look at the proposed domain name and realizes that the distinctive part of the name is "geezer," and that "sports" is a generic term. In other words, if there are other trademarks using "geezer," Steve should know about them, even if they don't also use "sports." Steve performs another search, this time using "geezer" in the top Search Term box and leaving the lower Search Term box blank. This time, the search turns up 19 items that use the word "geezer" (see Figure 4).

[Logout] *Please logout when you are done to release system resources allocated for you.*

[Start] List At: [   ] OR [Jump] to record: [   ]   19 Records(s) found (This page: 1 ~ 19)

	Serial Number	Reg. Number	Word Mark	Live/Dead Indicator
1	75770021		GEEZER.COM	DEAD
2	75614160		GEEZER WEAR	LIVE
3	75614155		GEEZER WEAR	LIVE
4	75885147		GIZMO GEEZER	LIVE
5	75540081		GEEZERS!	LIVE
6	75702390		GEEZER.COM	DEAD
7	75658345		GEEZERGRAM	LIVE
8	75514940		GEEZER DIVISION	DEAD
9	75137305	2157492	GEEZER GOLF	LIVE
10	75137304	2157491	EBENEZER GEEZER	LIVE
11	75111697		GEEZER GEAR	DEAD
12	75035871		GEEZER'S GUARANTEED OLE DE FART FARTLESS [FAT FREE] RECIPES ONLY BY GEEZER BREEZE	DEAD

Figure 4

Of the 19 entries (at the time we did the search), many are listed as "live" and a few are listed as "dead." Live means that the mark is either registered or pending registration whereas dead means that the mark used to be in the system as a registered or pending mark but has since been canceled or abandoned.

One of the live trademarks is Geezer Golf. Uh-oh. Steve clicks Geezer Golf and discovers that Geezer Golf was registered in three international trademark classes: 016 (Paper goods and printed matter), 028 (Toys and sporting goods) and 035 (Advertising and business services). This means that the line of Geezer Sports books that Steve and Bob had imagined would fall into at least two of the same classes as those for which Geezer Golf is registered. (For more information about the trademark classification system, see Chapter 7, Section B2.) Using geezersports.com might well confuse customers about articles sold on Bob and Steve's website and those identified by the existing trademark. (Customer confusion is discussed in Chapter 7.) This means that Bob and Steve probably couldn't get the name registered with the PTO—and even if they did, they might be sued for trademark infringement.

Alas, Steve and Bob give up on "Geezer Sports" but continue to enjoy their tennis rivalry. Maybe they'll come up with another clever name in the course of a particularly heated match. (After the first edition of this book was published, the company operating as Geezer Golf in Texas registered geezersports.com.)

8. Understanding the TESS Free Form Search

The TESS Free Form Search lacks the ease of the Structured Form Search but adds a substantial degree of flexibility. Let's first take a look at the Free Form Search (see Figure 5).

View Search History: [◆]
WARNING:
AFTER SEARCHING THE USPTO DATABASE, EVEN IF **YOU** THINK THE RESULTS ARE "O.K.," DO **NOT** ASSUME THAT
YOUR MARK CAN BE REGISTERED AT THE USPTO. AFTER YOU FILE AN APPLICATION, THE USPTO MUST DO ITS
OWN SEARCH AND OTHER REVIEW, AND MIGHT REFUSE TO REGISTER YOUR MARK.

Please enter search term in the field below:

Records
Returned: Plurals:
[50 ◆]   [No ◆]   Quick Tips

[⌃]
[⌄]
[Submit Query] [Clear Query]   [Logout] *Please logout when you are done to release system resources allocated for you.*

US Trademark Field Codes

Code & Name	Code & Name	Code & Name
[AD] Abandonment Date	[IC] International Class	[RE] Renewals
[AF] Affidavits	[IU] Filed ITU	[RG] Register
[AR] Assignment Recorded	[LD] Live/Dead	[RN] Registration Number

Figure 5

The Free Form Search page resembles the Structured Form Search page described in Section 5 above, with two major differences:

- Instead of separate Search Term boxes, the page provides one box which permits the construction of complex search queries, and
- The bottom of the page sets out the various fields that are available for searching and provides hypertext links to descriptions of these fields.

a. Using the Free Form Search Box

Probably the most important feature of the Free Form Search is that you can combine Boolean operators (unlike the Structured Search Form, which gives you only one Boolean operator for your entire query). For example, suppose your proposed domain name is MiracleMediations.com. You may have started out with the Structured Search Form entering "mirac*" in the top Search Term box and the term "mediat*" in the bottom box. You choose the AND operator to search for trademarks that contain both terms.

This search is a good start, but as you review your search results you realize that you want to search for trademarks that contain the word "arbitration" as well. To do this, you can use the Free Form Search to create a new search query that looks like this:

"mirac* [bi]" AND "mediat* [bi]" OR "arbitrat* [bi]"

This search expression tells the computer that you want all trademarks to appear which contain a variant of the truncated term "mirac*" and either the term "mediat*" or the term "arbitrat*," and it asks the computer to look for these terms in the Basic Index. The [bi] that follows the truncated terms is what's known as a field code, and the bi stands for Basic Index.

b. How to Use the Field Codes

As we explain above, the [bi] that follows the truncated terms is what's known as a field code. The Free Form Search requires the use of these field codes if you want anything other than an "all fields" search. For instance, if you want to search for all marks owned by a particular company, you can use the field code "[on]" (owner's name) for the company's name. Similarly, choosing the field code "[gs]" (goods and services) lets you search for all marks that are used on goods or services containing the terms you use in your search query.

You aren't limited to one field code. You may search in as many fields as you wish. For instance, you will get a deeper search by combining the [bi] (basic index) and [ti] (translation index) fields. The translation index is made up of variant terms that the PTO feels are close enough to registered or pending marks to warrant being automatically returned in any search made of the underlying mark. You combine fields for each term by separating the fields with a comma, as in geezer [bi,ti].

For more on field codes, use the table that appears on the Free Form Search page and click whatever field code you wish to know more about.

9. Understanding the Results of Your Search

It's one thing to search for marks using TESS; it's another to understand what is reported back to you. For example, when we clicked on the Geezer Golf item in our trademark search results, we get this page:

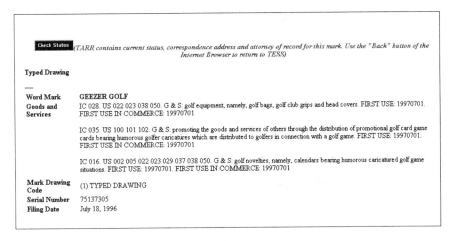

Figure 6

a. Understanding the Report Returned by a TESS Search

Let's take a few moments to interpret the various lines of information on the Geezer Golf page.

Word Mark: This shows the mark as registered (or as shown in the trademark application if the mark is pending).

Goods and Services: This line identifies the international classifications (the IC class) under which the mark is registered and provides brief descriptions of the underlying goods and/or services. In this case the mark is registered under international classifications 028, 035 and 016. The U.S. classifications following the international classification are artifacts of an earlier time when the U.S. had its own classification system. (See Chapter 7 where we explain the importance of classes in deciding whether there is a likelihood of customer confusion.)

Mark Drawing Code: If the mark consists of words only (even if they are imaginatively arranged or come with stylistic fonts), this line says "Typed Drawing." However, if the mark consists of a logo with graphical elements, this line will show a set of six numeric characters that reflect how the PTO has classified the logo.

Serial Number: This is the number that is assigned to the trademark application by the PTO.

Filing Date: This is the date that the application for registration was filed.

Files ITU: If the application was filed on an intent to use basis, that fact will be indicated here. If the application was filed on an actual use basis, this line will be blank. We can see here that this application was filed on an intent to use basis.

Published for Opposition: This line indicates the date the PTO published the trademark application to give the public a chance to oppose the mark (usually on grounds that they think the proposed registration legally conflicts with their trademark).

Registration Number: This line will only appear if the mark has, in fact, been registered. Pending marks, for instance, do not have a registration number.

Registration Date: This line will only appear if the mark has been registered.

Owner: This line identifies the person or entity that was named as owner of the trademark in the application, and also provides the owner's address.

Disclaimer: This line sets out any disclaimers that the applicant made in the course of getting the PTO to approve the application. The PTO commonly requires disclaimers where parts of the mark are common or generic terms, such as ".com." In this case, the applicant disclaims any ownership of the word golf, but retains the right of ownership to the term Geezer when used on goods or services described in the registration. This means that the company cannot prohibit another business from using "golf" as part of its trademark, but it can prohibit anyone from using "golf" in combination with "geezer."

Type of Mark: This line identifies the label given the mark by the PTO. For most purposes, this label makes little difference. However, if two potentially conflicting marks are very similar, but one is a service mark while the other is a trademark, the type of mark may make a difference in terms of whether a legal conflict exists.

Register: This line designates whether the mark has been registered on the Principal Register or the Supplemental Register. Marks on the Principal Register get full protection, whereas marks on the Supplemental Register are deemed by the PTO to be too descriptive to be placed on the Principal Register—which means that the likelihood of a successful infringement action being brought on behalf of that mark is small.

Live/Dead Indicator: This line indicates whether the mark is registered or pending, or whether it has been canceled (because of the owner's failure to renew or file statements of continued use) or abandoned in the course of the application.

⚠️ **Even though a mark is labeled as dead,** it may in fact be very much alive in the world of commerce and can spell trouble for you if you adopt a legally conflicting mark. The dead/live label only refers to the mark's status in the PTO, not to whether it is or isn't in actual use in the economy.

b. Determining a Mark's Status

Each item page, such as the one shown above for Geezer Golf, has a link to the PTO's Trademark Application Registration Retrieval database (known as TARR). This database shows the status of the mark (registered, pending, canceled, published for opposition, etc.). Here is what we get when we click the Status link to the geezer golf item page:

Thank you for your request. Here are the latest results from the TARR web server.

Serial Number: 75137305

Registration Number: 2157492

Mark (words only): GEEZER GOLF

Current Status: Registered.

Date of Status: 1998-05-12

Filing Date: 1996-07-18

Registration Date: 1998-05-12

Law Office Assigned: TMEG Law Office 109

CURRENT APPLICANT(S)/OWNER(S)

Figure 7

As you can see, this page has some of the same information as the item page and also provides a chronological history of the mark's journey through the PTO. This status report is most helpful when you discover a pending mark and want to know how far along it is in the process of registration.

D. Searching Online for Unregistered Trademarks

There is no list, anywhere, of unregistered trademarks as such. But by searching online, you can find product and service names that are trademarks being used by other businesses. As the percentage of businesses marketing their goods and services online approaches 100%, the ability to discover the real-world use of unregistered trademarks improves apace.

A good place to start is the Dot.com Directory at http://www.dotcomdirectory.com, a comprehensive listing of business websites. Simply enter the name of the product or service that you're looking for, and you will obtain a list of sites that have such products or services. This list may include some currently used commercial names that are the same as or similar to the one you want to use. Another good place to search for unregistered trademarks online is the Thomas Register of goods and services, at http://www.thomasregister.com.

Finally, you can simply enter the name in one of the Internet's many search engines and see what turns up. Although this type of search will produce all uses of the term, not just instances of use as a trademark, it may still produce some useful information.

E. Using a Trademark Search Service

Specialized trademark search firms traditionally conducted searches only for trademark attorneys. Even today, some of the largest trademark search firms refuse to conduct searches for anyone but a lawyer. But most search firms aren't so choosy and will conduct a search for anyone willing to pay.

1. Why Use a Search Service

Before putting a lot of time and money into promoting your website, you'll want to be as confident as possible that your domain name is "bulletproof" when it comes to trademark infringement claims. A search on the PTO's website as described in Section C, is a good start, but commercial firms will give you a better idea of whether your name will survive a conflict with a pending or registered mark. Most businesses adopt a cost/benefit approach and hire a search service to do a final trademark search.

Here are some of the things a commercial search service can do for you:

Obtain a search report that is completely up to date. The PTO's website is always a little behind. (The site tells you when the database was last updated and when the next update will be.) So if someone has filed an application to register a trademark very similar to your proposed domain name within the last few weeks, your search most likely won't pick it up. A lag time of a few weeks is tolerable to initially determine the legal viability of your proposed domain name, but you should definitely have an up-to-date search done before pouring money into promoting the domain name.

Search state (not just federal) trademark registration records. Every state allows the registration of marks that are used primarily in that state. If your choice for a domain name is the same or confusingly similar to one of these state-registered marks, you may run into trouble if the mark's owner decides to use the mark for a domain name, only to discover that you have registered it first. So it's always a good idea to run your choice by the list of state trademark registrations, something a commercial service can do for you more efficiently than you can do for yourself.

Locate variations on and fragments of the distinctive part of your name. Sometimes similarity in sound or appearance of just a portion of two names is enough to cause customer confusion. Experienced searchers have a knack for spotting potentially troublesome fragments and will probably do a better job of finding them than you would.

Search proprietary databases for unregistered marks. Over the years, commercial search firms have built their own private databases of business and product names and logos. These firms also have access to, and are adept at searching, the many hundreds of commercial databases available through Dialog and other online aggregators of data. A search of these databases may produce conflicts that you probably would not discover in your relatively disorganized search for unregistered marks, whether you searched online or in a library. Although most of these databases are available to the general public, you must pay either a subscription or one-time use fee, and learning to use them requires some effort.

> *Trademark: Legal Care for Your Business & Product Name,* by Stephan Elias (Nolo), a good place to start if you want to do your own comprehensive search.

2. Cost Factors

You can hire either a trademark search firm or a trademark lawyer to handle a search for you.

Because only attorneys are allowed to offer legal advice about potential trademark conflicts, trademark search services offered by attorneys tend to cost the most. If you hire a trademark attorney to advise you on the choice and registration of a domain name, the attorney can arrange for the trademark search. Some attorneys do it themselves, but most farm the search out to a search firm. Once the report comes back from the search firm, the attorney will interpret it for you and advise you on whether to go ahead with your proposed domain name.

Trademark search firms offer many different levels of services, and their fees vary accordingly. The price often depends on how much handling the information receives before it is delivered to you. Generally, raw data is cheap; highly processed and organized data is more expensive. For instance, if the search just involves running one proposed domain name past the PTO's database, the cost usually will be less than $50. But if you want the searcher to seek out registered trademarks that in whole or in part might resemble your name in meaning, sound and appearance, then the cost increases as the labor required does. If you also want the search to include an intensive hunt for unregistered marks, you are getting up into the several-hundred-dollars range.

The difference in rates among search firms may also reflect variations in the coverage of the search, the type of report you receive, the experience of the searchers or simply economies of scale. Some firms may advertise an unusually low price to draw in customers, but then add on charges that end up exceeding another firm's total price—a professional version of bait-and-switch advertising. To shop sensibly, you need to know the total cost of each service, so be sure to ask questions before committing yourself. For example, does one fee cover the whole cost, or is there also a per-page charge for the report?

3. Finding a Service

There are many trademark search services in this country. You don't have to worry much about where a particular service is located—phone, fax and email make it possible for a customer in Bangor, Maine, to comfortably deal with a service in Austin, Texas. But if you want a local service, consult the phone book or an electronic "Yellow Pages" such as those offered by Yahoo!, Netscape and the major search engines. Although some trademark search firms limit their services to lawyers, most also perform searches for individuals and businesses.

Some trademark search services will try to convince you that you're stupid if you don't search every corner of the globe for possible conflicts. Don't just agree; make an independent decision about what scope of search is appropriate for you. Also, some search services provide additional services, such as the preparation of applications for federal and state trademark registrations. Like trademark lawyers, these businesses have a vested interest in convincing you that you will be better served by paying them to handle the tasks in question than by doing them yourself. If you feel that this point of view—which may in some cases be perfectly reasonable—is being too aggressively pushed, get a firm hold on your wallet and consider finding another service.

SILICON VALLEY SEARCHERS

California's Silicon Valley is home to the Sunnyvale Center on Innovation, Invention and Ideas, or Sc[i]3 (pronounced Sigh-Cubed). It is one of three Patent and Trademark Depository Libraries—the others are in Detroit and Houston—that have formed partnerships with the U.S. Patent and Trademark Office. Under this partnership, these libraries are encouraged to offer a variety of information services, including trademark searches, for very reasonable fees, usually a notch or two below those charged by commercial firms.

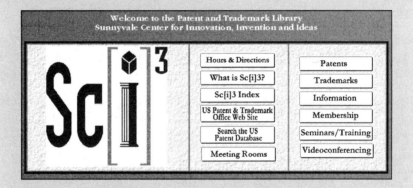

Sc[I]3 offers searches of varying scope. Like most trademark search firms, Sc[i]3 doesn't interpret its results; it leaves that to you. Your basic task is to review the trademarks that Sc[I]3 turns up in its search and compare them to your domain name for the likelihood of customer confusion. (Chapter 7 helps you do this.) You can order a Sc[i]3 trademark search by calling 408-730-7290. Visit www.sci3.com for a current list of services and fees. You can get the results of the search within 24 hours if you are willing to pay a premium. Otherwise it takes a little longer.

You may also find help with your trademark search by physically visiting one of the other 80-plus Patent and Trademark Depository Libraries located throughout the United States. These libraries usually offer excellent reference services for people doing their own research. Visit http://www.uspto.gov and click Libraries-PTDLs on the home page for a complete list of locations and contact information.

F. Assessing Your Search Results

Once you've carried out your trademark search, you'll have several options, depending on the results.

If your search turned up no results, your search parameters were probably too narrow. You should rethink your search strategy and try again. Although it's possible that no existing trademarks exactly match your proposed domain name, it's virtually impossible that there aren't some marks that are at least close.

If your search turns up trademarks that you think might conflict with your proposed domain name, your next step is to go to Chapter 7. You will be looking for the answer to one question: Would the use of your domain name create the likelihood of customer confusion between the products or services on your website and those identified by an existing mark? If you answer yes, you might well be guilty of trademark infringement if you go ahead and use the domain name you're considering.

If you conclude that your domain name won't infringe another business's trademark, your next step is to consider registering the domain name with the PTO as a trademark. We explain that process in Chapter 8. ■

CHAPTER 7

How to Tell Whether Customer Confusion Is Likely

You need to consider the issue of customer confusion if you have run your proposed domain name through a trademark search and found that a similar name—one that resembles yours in sound, appearance or meaning—is already being used by another business on or offline. Whether or not you should go ahead with your name depends on whether doing so would create a likelihood of customer confusion. If there is a likelihood of confusion, you risk being sued for trademark infringement if you use the name. If customer confusion isn't likely—for example, Delta Airlines and Delta faucets have coexisted peacefully for years—you can go ahead with the name.

⚠ If your search has turned up a famous mark that is similar to your proposed domain name, you should proceed with caution. Famous marks are entitled to be free from other uses that would dilute their strength or tarnish their reputation for quality—whether or not such uses result in customer confusion.

A. What Constitutes Customer Confusion

The phrase "likelihood of confusion" is the key to most trademark conflicts. A "likelihood" means that confusion is probable—not necessarily that it has happened, or that it will happen, but that it is more likely than not that a reasonable customer would be confused by the simultaneous use of the two names.

Confusion in this context can mean two different things. Most commonly, it means that the goods or services a customer buys are different than what the customer intended to buy. For instance, suppose, on the recommendation of a friend, that you decide to purchase Lee's famous Flamebrain barbecue sauce, which is only sold online. You intend to type "flamebrain.com" into your browser but accidentally enter "flamerbrain.com" instead. You get a website run by Henry, who has both copied Lee's idea to offer a barbecue sauce for sale online and, with a very minor variation, the name of Lee's sauce. You order two bottles, completely unaware that you ordered the wrong product from the wrong website.

The other kind of customer confusion occurs when a misleading name causes customers to believe—wrongly—that a product or service is sponsored by, approved of or somehow connected with a business they already know about. In other words, customers are confused about the source of the product or service. This would be the case, for example, if you took your TV to a repair shop called IBM Electronics because you thought that IBM somehow sponsored the business.

The law imagines a "reasonable" customer who exercises ordinary care to distinguish among products and services. Courts recognize that a reasonable consumer will often make a snap judgment. For example, if, after only a hurried glance, you are confused between Heartbeat and Heartlite cooking oils, then the marks are too similar. That's reasonable. However, the law surely would not find it reasonable if you confused Heartbeat cooking oil with Esther's Cooking Oil because your Aunt Esther had recently died of a heart attack. Nor would it be reasonable to confuse Heartbeat with Esther's because of similar packaging, so long as the very different names were prominently displayed on the packaging.

In *Goto.com v. Walt Disney Co.*, 202 F.3d 1199 (9th Cir., 2000), the Ninth Circuit Court of Appeals found that clicking on a link takes little effort and is unlikely to involve a great deal of care. In other words, the court held that the argument that consumers may often make snap judgments is especially applicable to the Internet.

Someone who alleges a trademark infringement must show (if the dispute goes to court) that a reasonable customer might be confused by the simultaneous use of the two marks. Typically, the challenger must show that a significant percentage of customers would likely be confused—anywhere between 5% and 50%, depending on the situation.

The percentage varies from one court decision to the next. Proof typically comes in the form of statistically valid surveys and focus groups and occasionally in cases of actual confusion.

Watch your metatags. Metatags are brief descriptions and key words that are pulled from a website's content and made part of the website's code. Users don't see this code, but it is visible to search engines. As a general rule, metatags should consist only of descriptive terms—ordinary terms that define your site's content—rather than distinctive terms that are in use by competing websites.

A court recently ruled that metatags that initially divert people away from a website containing a registered trademark may violate the trademark owner's rights. (*Brookfield Communications, Inc. v. West Coast Entertainment Corporation*, 174 F.3d 1036 (9th Cir. 1999).) If your metatags have this effect, you could be forced to change them.

For example, suppose Josh launches a website for buying and selling Pokemon cards. Pokemon is a registered trademark of Nintendo of America, Inc., which operates pokemon.com. If Josh uses the word pokemon as a metatag, he might run afoul of Nintendo's trademark rights and end up at the wrong end of a court order forcing him to get rid of the metatags and perhaps pay money damages to Nintendo.

However, another court recently ruled that a company's trademark was not infringed by an independently operated website, which served as a complaint center directed at the company, even though the website used the company's mark in its metatags. The court found that the use did not create a likelihood of customer confusion and was a fair use of the mark rather than a trademark infringement. (*Bihari and Bihari Interiors, Inc. v. Gross*, 119 F.Supp.2d 309 (S.D.N.Y. 2000).)

B. Factors to Consider When Evaluating Potential Customer Confusion

Over the years, the courts have developed various tests for deciding whether or not there is a likelihood of confusion between two marks. According to the Goto.com case (see Section A, above), three criteria are paramount when determining whether a likelihood of customer confusion exists with respect to two marks that are both used online:

- whether the marks are similar
- whether the underlying goods or services are related, and
- whether the marks are simultaneously being used in the same marketing channel.

Although the Goto.com case involved conflicting logos rather than domain names, the court's reasoning easily can be applied to domain name disputes.

1. How Similar Are the Marks?

The first factor in determining whether the use of a domain name will cause a likelihood of confusion is how similar the name is to an existing trademark. Do they sound or look alike, and if so, how much? Do they convey the same meaning? The closer two names are in sight, sound and meaning, the more likely it is that a legal problem will arise. For example, trains4travel.com and trainsfortravel.com would obviously create confusion in the marketplace.

Even marks with greater differences may create the likelihood of customer confusion in the same market. Courts have found that Quirst is too close to Squirt, Sarnoff too much like Smirnoff, Lorraine too reminiscent of La Touraine. Each of these pairs of names were used on nearly identical goods. Probably the use of such close names would have passed legal muster if they had been on very different kinds of products.

But the more that competitive names are in the same class or market channels, the less similar the names have to be to cause confusion.

2. Are the Goods or Services Closely Related?

When similar names are used on related goods or services, the risk of consumer confusion is high. You can determine whether goods or services are related by asking these questions:

a. Do the Goods or Services Compete?

Goods and services directly compete if the purchase of one negatively affects the purchase of the other. If the goods or services offered on your website directly compete with goods or services identified by an existing mark, a court would probably find that the goods or services are related.

b. Do They Belong to the Same Class of Goods or Services?

The U.S. Patent and Trademark Office puts every new trademark in one or more "international classes," which are categories of goods and services. There are 42 classes in all, 34 for products and eight for services. The Appendix contains a complete list of the classes and descriptions of each.

Goods or services within the same class are likely to be related either because they compete with each other or are marketed in the same channels.

Most commercial websites offer services, especially information services. Other examples of online services are investing, auctions, entertainment and retail (for instance, Amazon.com provides a retail service even though it sells a wide variety of goods carrying their own marks).

How can you tell what class a possibly conflicting mark belongs in? When you do a trademark search (described in Chapter 6), the search results will show what class or classes have been assigned to the marks that turn up. If the goods or services offered on your website belong in the same class as those of another business, this is a pretty good indication that the services will be considered related.

Example 1: *The owner of megasoft.com, a developer of downloadable software, wants to sue the owner of megasoft.net to stop it from selling its own custom-developed downloadable software under the name megasoft. Both names fall into Class 9 for downloadable software. The owner who was first to use the mark for selling downloadable software would likely prevail if the dispute reached court.*

Example 2: *Software developer megasoft.com probably couldn't stop a maker of ultra-soft, custom-knit blankets, (Class 24, Fabrics), from using the name megasoft.net to sell its blankets over the Web. Downloadable software and blankets don't compete in any way; they are not considered related goods, and the megasoft mark could be used on both without creating the likelihood of customer confusion.*

By itself, the fact that two products or services are in the same class does not conclusively establish that two names are legally in conflict. The classification system packs all goods and services into only 42 classes—combining, for example, abrasive cleansers and cosmetics—so products within the same class may be marketed in totally different ways so as to avoid customer confusion. You certainly could argue that a trademark for a scouring powder that is similar to a trademark for lipstick wouldn't confuse customers.

To classify your own product or service, study the list of classes in the Appendix. The choice may be obvious; if it isn't, look at the examples for each class. If you are still not sure, pick the three most likely classes and use them as possibilities.

3. Are the Marks Used in the Same Marketing Channel?

When similar marks are used in the same marketing channel, the likelihood of customer confusion is high. Traditionally, this issue looks to whether customers are likely to encounter or learn about the different products or services in the same store, catalog, advertising or other means of promotion or distribution. If so, then they would be more likely to think the goods or services are associated in some way. If, on the other hand, the goods or services were marketed quite differently, then no confusion would be likely to exist.

The presence of portals (Yahoo!, AOL), search engines (Google, AltaVista) and electronic product catalogs and indexes make it likely that the simultaneous use of similar marks anywhere online for related goods or services will lead to customer confusion as to their source or sponsor. In other words, the Internet can be seen as one large marketing channel that makes conflicting marks much more likely to cause customer confusion than they would be in the "brick and mortar" world.

4. Other Customer Confusion Factors

If a conflict exists between a trademark that is not used online and a domain name (which, needless to say, is used online), the marketing channels are different and additional criteria may be applied to decide whether customer confusion is likely. These additional criteria have traditionally focused on:

- the strength of the trademark that is allegedly being infringed
- the cost of the goods or services (the more expensive they are, the more likely that consumers will take care and avoid confusion)
- whether the owner of the mark is likely to expand into different products or services

- the alleged infringer's intent
- whether proof of actual customer confusion exists, and
- whether the disputing parties share the same customer base.

Let's take a closer look at these additional criteria.

a. Is the Other Trademark Strong?

You are safer in using a name that is similar to an existing weak trademark than one that is similar to an existing strong trademark. A mark is considered strong either because:

- the words, phrases, or symbols it consists of are inherently distinctive (arbitrary, coined or suggestive), or
- long and continuous use has made the public recognize it as the symbol of a particular product or service (it has acquired a secondary meaning, also sometimes referred to as acquired distinctiveness).

The weaker a name is, the less legal protection it is given, and the more likely it is that your domain name will be found to not be confusingly similar, even if it has many similarities.

Example: *New Legal Solutions, Inc., wants to use the domain name webdocs.com for its website, which offers electronic forms. However, a trademark search discloses that the term "Webdocs" is registered on the Federal Principal Trademark Register. New Legal Solutions is surprised at the registration, because Webdocs appears to be too descriptive to qualify for the Principal Register (see Chapter 8). New Legal Solutions decides to run a search for Webdocs on the Internet. The search engine returns hits for 150 different websites that use Webdocs for the same purpose intended by New Legal Solutions.*

Because the term is in such general use, and therefore legally weak as a trademark, New Legal Solutions decides to go ahead and use it as a domain name. The trademark owner may technically have an infringement claim against New Legal Solutions, but New Legal Solutions would have a strong defense, which is the mark's lack of distinctiveness due to its highly descriptive quality and its widespread use throughout the Internet. (Using the name, however, is probably not the best choice, for other reasons discussed in Chapter 4.)

b. Are the Goods or Services Expensive?

Because customers tend to take their time and consider carefully when buying an expensive item, the more expensive the item, the less chance of confusing customers. An item that is cheap or likely to be bought on impulse, however, is more likely to result in customer confusion if it is sold with a mark that is similar to another on goods that are even slightly related.

c. Is the Senior User Likely to Expand Into Different Products or Services?

A red flag should go up if the potentially conflicting name has already been used on a variety of products or services by the same business, even if you wish to use it on a product that is unrelated to any of these uses. An owner who uses the name on several products or services has what is called in legal lingo the "right of expansion." Some examples of businesses that do this are Calvin Klein and Pierre Cardin, who have expanded from clothing to fragrances, accessories and other products.

The rationale for this rule is that the public, having seen a name on a variety of goods made by the same company, is likely to assume that any new uses also belong to that company, and thus are likely to be confused. For example, the public would expect the name *Yamaha*, which already appears on motorcycles, lawnmowers and guitars, to represent the same company if it also appeared on computers or musical recordings.

Courts also assume that the first user may wish to expand the name's use further, and they protect this right of expansion by permitting very few other uses of the same name. So a second business seeking to use such a name, even on greatly dissimilar products, will have less luck than if the name were being used in a more limited fashion.

d. What Was the Alleged Infringer's Intent?

Courts also judge the intent of the alleged infringer in a likelihood of confusion analysis. If it appears probable to the court that a business could only have chosen its mark in order to take advantage of its similarity to another mark, then the court is very likely to find an infringement to exist. If, for example, a successful and well-known marketer of French bread uses *Staff of Life* as a trademark, and a new rival calls its product *Staff of Life*, the court will be very suspicious about the intent of the rival—and it may be hard to persuade the judge or jury that the owner of the *Staff of Life* mark did not intentionally copy the first mark.

e. Does Proof of Actual Customer Confusion Exist?

Evidence of actual cases of customer confusion is not necessary to prove trademark infringement, but such proof can be particularly compelling. Diversion of sales or damage to one's reputation or goodwill can show that actual confusion has occurred. And this can have a strong effect on a likelihood of confusion analysis. The confusion need not be based on completed transactions; it can be shown by inquiries, such as phone calls placed to the wrong party because of the similarity of names. Presumably, customers who have looked for a particular company but inadvertently clicked on a similar domain name can constitute proof of actual confusion.

f. Do Your Businesses Share the Same Customer Base?

Two businesses that use similar names to sell to the same customers are highly likely to cause customer confusion. But if businesses have separate customer bases, then the use of similar names is unlikely to confuse anyone. For example, the market for replacement wood windows is likely to be limited to contractors and homeowners with spare cash. As a result, a window manufacturer who uses the domain name WallsofLight.com and the same name in its advertising probably won't confuse the customers of a climbing gym supplier that calls its special demonstration the Wall of Lights. The two groups of customers don't overlap.

It's useful to look at how large a sector of the market uses your product or service. If a small sector of the market knows and purchases a service, a similar mark used by a different small group is unlikely to confuse the two sets of consumers. But if a large segment of the public knows one name, use of a similar name is more likely to cause customer confusion, even if aimed at a slightly different market, because of the greater potential for overlap between the two groups.

As we have pointed out, the Internet has created one customer base for all goods or services being distributed through e-commerce. Accordingly, this criterion is likely to be of little significance unless, again, one of the parties has no intention of doing commerce online. Furthermore, many courts no longer view the question of customer base as a separate factor and instead review it as part of the marketing channel analysis.

If you're worried about infringement—yours or someone else's—the advice of an experienced attorney can be very helpful. Courts resolve trademark disputes on a case-by-case basis, and someone who has studied a variety of cases should have an informed opinion. See Chapter 9 for advice on how to find a trademark attorney. ■

CHAPTER 8

How to Register Your Domain Name As a Trademark

Being the first to use a trademark—not registering it—makes you the owner of a trademark. But registering your trademark with the U.S. Patent and Trademark Office will make it easier for you to enforce your legal rights as a trademark owner because it makes you the *presumed* owner of the trademark. If a dispute over the trademark arises, and a lawsuit is filed, it will be up to the other party to convince the court that you are not the owner.

In addition, once your mark is registered, every later user is presumed to know about it. Any infringement by them will be presumed deliberate, making you eligible for triple damages (three times the amount of money you actually lose as a result of the infringement), profits earned by the defendant as a result of the infringement, and possibly attorney fees. If you can't sue for these enhanced damages, you may well have trouble finding an attorney to take your case without a very large retainer fee. And if you can't find an attorney, you may well have trouble enforcing your rights as a trademark owner.

This chapter explains how to file your trademark application online. If you need more help once your application is filed, check the resources discussed at the end of this chapter.

A. Applying for Registration: An Overview

Filling out and filing a trademark application for your domain name with the U.S. Patent and Trademark Office is a snap. The PTO website offers two online application programs, called e-TEAS and PrinTEAS. According to the PTO, it shouldn't take you more than 20 minutes to complete the application.

The filing fee for registering most domain name marks is $325. It can go up if your website will be offering a number of different types of services.

To complete the registration process, you must actually be using the domain name on a website. However, you can start the application process on the ground that you intend to use the name in the near future (called an intent-to-use application). If you go on to actually use the name and complete the registration process, your application date will also be considered the date of first use for the mark, which will give you a priority claim over later users. (See Chapter 3 for more on trademark ownership priorities.)

Although it's easy and quick to apply for trademark registration, the processing of your application can take a year or more. The PTO is overbooked and understaffed these days. In the meantime, your actual or intended domain name will appear in the PTO's trademark database as a pending trademark. Anyone doing a trademark search (see Chapter 6) will find your name and know that you are claiming it as a trademark. This in itself gives you a lot of protection because it will deter others from pursuing your name as a trademark.

B. What Domain Names May Be Registered As Trademarks

Not all domain names may be registered as trademarks. The PTO appears to be unwilling to register generic domain names, such as coffee.com or drugs.com. Similarly, the PTO will look askance at weak domain names, such as those using a surname or descriptive terms. (Chapter 3 discusses the difference between distinctive (strong) marks, descriptive (weak) marks and generic terms.)

Even weak marks, however, can usually make it on to what's called the supplemental register. So if the PTO rejects your original application because your mark lacks distinctiveness, you can amend the application and ask that the mark be added to the supplemental register. The supplemental register doesn't provide the same benefits as the main trademark register (called the Principal Register), but it does put your mark on the map, so people will find it when they do a trademark search. At the very least, you will prevent unknowing infringement of your domain name.

Federal rules prohibit certain types of trademarks from being registered at all. There haven't been any court decisions on how these rules apply to domain names, but existing trademark law suggests that the following types of domain names are not registrable:

- Domain names that contain "immoral," "deceptive" or "scandalous" matter. Immoral or scandalous, in this context, means that the mark might cause scandal or be disgraceful, offensive, disreputable, or excite retribution or elicit condemnation from the average consumer. These rather loose guidelines are considered in light of the mark itself and with the goods or services to which it is attached. There aren't any recently decided court cases on this subject, but you can imagine that some four-letter words with a .com after them are not going to be accepted by the PTO. A deceptive mark is one that suggests that the product or service came from a source other than its true source—for example, a domain name such as californiacheese.com, which only sells cheese from Wisconsin. (The PTO uses the sample of your trademark, which you are required to submit along with your application (called the specimen) to make sure that, among other things, your name is not deceptive. See Section D, below for more about specimens.)

- Domain names that disparage or falsely suggest a connection with persons (living or dead), institutions, beliefs or national symbols. For example, the domain name jackieofashions.com would not be a registrable trademark for a website that attempts to use Jackie Onassis's image to sell clothing totally unconnected with the former first lady or her estate.

- Domain names that consist of or contain a name identifying a particular living individual (except with his or her written consent), or the name of a deceased president of the United States during the life of his widow, if any, except with the written consent of the widow. For example, you may be able to register the domain name barbrastreisand.com, but the PTO won't register it as a trademark for a website that sells Barbra Streisand CDs, photos, dolls, plates and other memorabilia, unless Barbra Streisand gives you written consent to use her name.

- Domain names containing marks that organizations have the exclusive right, by statute, to use. Boy Scouts is a good example. Similarly, use of the name Smokey the Bear is reserved to the Department of the Interior. So boyscouts.com and smokeythebear.com are off-limits as trademarks.

C. Different Ways to Register, Online and Off

The PTO now offers a quick and easy way to file a trademark registration application online. There are actually two systems available on the PTO website: e-TEAS and PrinTEAS. This book takes you through e-TEAS, which is a fully electronic system, allowing you to both fill in and file your application to the PTO online. PrinTEAS allows you to fill in the application online, but you must print out your filled-in application and send it to the PTO through the regular mail. If you decide to use PrinTEAS, you can easily adapt our instructions to fill in the application, and we provide instructions for mailing the application to the PTO.

Which program should you choose? It's faster and cheaper to use e-TEAS, because you don't have to pay for postage. One possible barrier to using e-TEAS, however, is the "specimen" requirement. If you are filing on the basis that you are already using the domain name (called an "actual use" application), you will have to submit a electronic file showing your domain name in actual use. (For more on specimen requirements, see Section D, below.) This entails capturing your image in jpeg or gif format using a graphics program like *Adobe Illustrator* or *Photoshop, ImageStyler, AppleWorks, SimpleImage* or *Microsoft ImageReady*. If you don't have this type of software, or you are graphics-software challenged, you can always use PrinTEAS and accompany your application with a hard copy of your chosen specimen. There's one more wrinkle. If you are using a Macintosh computer, you will need *Netscape Navigator* to fully operate e-TEAS. Microsoft's *Internet Explorer* for Macintosh will not allow a proper image attachment. If you are filing on an "intent to use" basis, you won't have to worry about sending a jpeg or gif file.

 If you want to fill out the application form on paper, you can download it from the PTO's website.

D. How to Use e-TEAS to Register Online

Using e-TEAS can be fun. It sure beats trying to file the paper form. Just follow along with our step-by-step instructions below. If you need additional help, the PTO provides help links.

Go to the PTO's website.

Your first step is to go to the PTO's website at http://www.uspto.gov. On the left side of the home page, click the "Trademark Electronic Business Center" icon. It will take you to the following page:

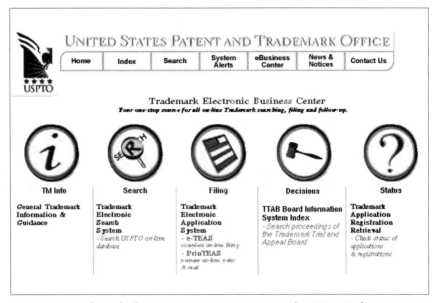

Trademark Electoronic Business Center, at the PTO's Website.

Click the filing icon.

That link takes you to this page.

TEAS Home Page

As you can see, you must choose between e-TEAS and PrinTEAS. If you scroll down the page, you'll find out which versions of *Netscape Navigator* and Microsoft *Internet Explorer* to use and how to contact the PTO for help.

Click the e-TEAS link.

You will get the Form Selection page.

Trademark Electronic Application System ®

NOTE: Effective August 1, 2000, the USPTO will no longer mail a paper filing receipt for electronically-submitted applications. The email summary of the application data will serve as your official filing receipt.

Please click on the following to access a form for:

■ Trademark/Servicemark Application, Principal Register
Use this form to file an initial application for either a trademark (used or intended to be used for goods) OR a servicemark (used or intended to be used in providing a service). If you use this application to file based on a 'bona fide intent to use' the mark some time in the future, i.e., the applicant has not actually used the mark yet in commerce, but can claim in good faith that it plans to do so later, you must also file a second form (the Statement of Use/ Amendment to Allege Use, below) before we can register the mark (even though otherwise approved based on the information in the original Trademark/Servicemark application). The filing fee is $325.00 per class of goods and/or services (i.e., if an application is for one mark, but it is used for computer software in Class 9 and t-shirts in Class 25, the filing fee is $650.00). Only one mark is permissible per application, although a mark may consist of several elements that are joined to form a composite whole (e.g., words plus a design). Also, the filing fee is a processing fee for the application. This fee is **NOT** returned even if ultimately the USPTO does not issue a registration. You should take all necessary steps to ensure the mark is registrable before filing the application.

NOTE: Electronic forms do not currently exist for the following: Application on the Supplemental Register; Application for a Certification Mark; Application for a Collective Trademark/Servicemark; Application for a Collective Membership Mark. For the last three, please see http://www.uspto.gov/web/forms/index.html#TM.

E-TEAS Home Page

Select "Trademark/Service Mark Application, Principal Register.

You will then be presented with the e-TEAS form wizard. Although you can switch from the wizard to the document itself, use of the wizard is recommended.

e-TEAS
Version 1.21 : 01/10/2000

Please answer all of the questions below to create an application form showing only sections relevant to you. Then press the NEXT button. For more information regarding any of the following questions or topics, either go to **HELP** or click on the underlined word. We strongly recommend that you use this WIZARD, but to skip, click on Standard Form.

PLEASE NOTE:

HELP instructions for each section of this form are available by simply clicking on the relevant words or box. While the different sections of the form may appear straightforward and easy to fill out, you are strongly advised to read the HELP instructions very carefully for EACH section PRIOR to actually completing it. Failure to follow this advice may cause you to fill out sections of the form incorrectly, jeopardizing your legal rights.

Once you submit an application, either electronically or through the mail, we will not cancel the filing or refund your fee, unless the application fails to satisfy minimum filing requirements. The fee is a processing fee, which we do not refund even if we cannot issue a registration after our substantive review.

1. What is your filing basis?

Intent to Use (Section 1(b))

● Yes ○ No

Use in Commerce (Section 1(a))

○ Yes ● No

Right of Priority based on Foreign Application (Section 44(d))

○ Yes ● No

Foreign Registration (Section 44(e))

○ Yes ● No

2. Are your Goods and/or Services in more than one class?

○ Yes ● No
If the answer is Yes, enter the number of classes [⬍]

3. How are you paying the application filing fee?

● Credit Card
○ Deposit Account

4. Does more than one applicant own the mark?

○ Yes ● No
If the answer is Yes, enter the number of owners [⬍]

e-TEAS Form Wizard

Question 1: What is your filing basis? If you are already using the domain name on your website and selling goods or services, select "use in commerce." If you are not yet up and running, select "intent to use."

The procedures for each basis are somewhat different, and the "intent to use" basis will cost you an additional $100 when you do put the domain name into actual use.

Previous Foreign Registration. If you are filing in the U.S. on the basis of a previous foreign registration, see a lawyer before continuing. This book doesn't cover U.S. registrations based on foreign registrations.

Question 2: Are your goods or services in more than one class? The PTO categorizes trademarks in 42 different classes based on the goods and services the business offers. To see which classes your goods and services belong in, check the list of classes in Appendix 2. In Appendix 3, you'll find a PTO circular that discusses which classes are appropriate for certain computer-related goods and services ("Identification and Classification of Certain Computer-Related Goods and Services").

If the type of good or service being offered by your website clearly fits within one of the classes described by the PTO, go ahead and enter the class number in the blank. If you think you fit in two or more classes, you can use this application to register under the additional classes. The more classes you register under, the broader your protection is likely to be. (See Chapter 7.) However, you must pay a filing fee of $325 for each additional class. So if money is an issue, pick the best class and use that for your initial registration. You can always file applications for additional classes down the road.

If your goods or services do not match the descriptions given in the PTO circular, try checking the "Trademark Acceptable Identification of Goods and Services Manual" on the PTO's website. Just click on the "Trademark" link from the PTO's home page. The next screen will show three columns. The first column is for trademark resources. Click "Trademark Acceptable Identification of Goods and Services Manual." The best way to use the manual is to use the search feature. Click "Search" and use keywords to find the list of goods or services that best describe your particular goods or services. For example, if you're going to use your trademark to identify your line of roasted coffee beans, type in "coffee" and click "Search" to find a list of coffee and coffee-related products from the Manual. This list will give you the PTO's suggested class number for your coffee beans. The PTO's list will also include descriptions, which you can use later on in the application.

If you can't choose a class, all is not lost. You can skip this part of the application, and the trademark examiner assigned to your application will contact you later with some suggestions. Who says government isn't friendly?

Question 3: How are you paying the application filing fee? This one is easy. You'll probably be paying with a credit card. Deposit accounts are usually used only by law firms and other businesses that register a lot of trademarks.

Question 4: Does more than one applicant own the mark? The applicant is the person or business that will own the trademark. If at all possible, only one person or business entity should own the domain name. This can be an individual, a partnership, a corporation, a limited liability company or a joint venture. If your situation dictates that there be two or more owners, click "more than one owner" and read the instructions.

Question 5: Is there one applicant, but more than one signatory? If there is a single applicant, only one person is needed to sign the application. If the applicant is a corporation, and corporate policy dictates that two or more officers sign the application, then enter the appropriate number here. If there is more than one applicant, then at least one person for each applicant must sign the application.

Question 6: Is an attorney filing this application? If you plan to be represented by an attorney in your dealings with the PTO, click "attorney." The PTO will not communicate directly with you if an attorney is representing you.

Question 7: Is the applicant's address outside the United States? If you live outside the U.S., click "applicant's address" for more information.

Question 8: Do You Need to Enter an Additional Statement? You can safely answer no to this request. About the only statement that might be relevant is what's called the disclaimer. This means that if you are using common, generic or descriptive words as part of your domain name, the PTO will want you to disclaim (give up) trademark rights in those specific words, even though you have a trademark in the name as a whole. For example, suppose you manufacture a highly successful line of perfume called Candor, and you wish to register the domain name candorperfume.com. The PTO will likely ask you to disclaim the word "perfume" because it is generic. The word "candor," however, is still registrable as a trademark for a line of perfume. That's OK since those generic words can't be registered or protected anyway. The trademark examiner will tell you somewhere in the process what words you should disclaim, so there is no point in doing it on the application.

Click next

You will be taken to the screen shown below.

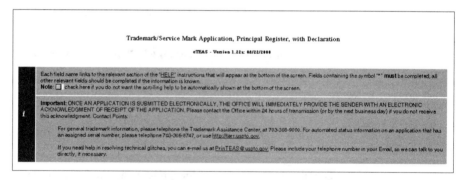

e-TEAS Standard Application Form, Showing Help Instructions

Carefully read the information at the top of this page. The first block explains the help system and lets you turn off the help text that automatically appears at the bottom of the page. It also explains that only the blanks marked with an asterisk are mandatory. We strongly recommend that you be as complete as possible in your responses, even if the information isn't mandatory; it may save you time and trouble down the line. Some of the non-mandatory information may be useful to the examiner in evaluating your application and expeditiously communicating with you if a problem arises. For example, your phone number isn't mandatory—but how will the examiner call you if you don't include it?

The name, entity, address, email address, fax number and phone number blanks all come with excellent help should you need it.

The next part of the application is the "Mark Information" box, as shown below:

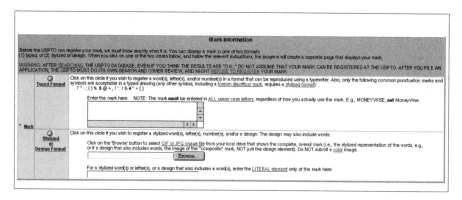

e-TEAS Standard Application Form, Showing Mark Information

Mark Information: Click the first circle above the words "Typed Format." Because you are registering a domain name, your trademark consists solely of words and numbers and will be displayed in what's called "typed drawing format." In the box just below the words "Enter the mark here," enter your domain name in all upper-case letters. You can enter the complete domain name, including the .com, or just the unique part of your name. For instance, Nolo might choose to register its domain name as NOLO.COM or just NOLO. Because domain names are such a new species of trademark, there are no firm rules.

The next part of the application is the "Basis for Filing and Goods and/or Services Information" box, as shown below:

BASIS FOR FILING AND GOODS AND/OR SERVICES INFORMATION
☒ Section 1(b), Intent to Use: Applicant has a bona fide intention to use or use through a related company the mark in commerce on or in connection with the goods and/or services identified below (15 U.S.C. §1051(b)).
International Class · · · · · · · If known, enter class number 001 - 042, A, B, or 200
* Listing of Goods and/or Services · · · · USPTO Goods/Services Manual

eTEAS Standard Application Form, Showing Basis for Filing

The appearance of this page will depend on what you indicated earlier in the wizard portion of the application. If you indicated that you are filing on an intent-to-use basis, this box will simply ask you to provide a class number and a description of the underlying goods or services for which your mark will be used. If you earlier indicated that you are filing on an "actual use" basis, this box will ask you to attach a specimen for each class under which you are registering. It also will ask for information as to your first use of the mark anywhere, and its first use in commerce that Congress may regulate, as well as the class number and description of the goods or services.

Specimens: If you're filing under Section 1(a) Use in Commerce, you'll need to provide a specimen image file and a description of the specimen in the next box. If you're an "intent to use" applicant, you will not have a specimen information section on your application and should go to International Class, below.

Your specimen must be a file in jpeg or gif format. If you are registering your entire domain name, it should be a copy of your website showing your domain name. Or, if you are just registering the unique part of your domain name (without the .com), your specimen may be an advertisement of your services. Either way, make sure your specimen shows your name exactly as you described it in the "mark" box above

Your specimen must show two things:

1) You are using your domain name as a trademark. A specimen that shows your website and the domain name typed into the address line of your browser is not sufficient. Your domain name should be a prominent part of the design of your home page. Ideally, it should be at the very top of the page, easy to spot and easy to read, and it should dominate the quadrant of the page in which it is located.

2) The services being offered on your website match the description of the services in your application. If you are providing financial information as your service, for example, make sure your specimen shows that you are doing so.

The next part of the specimen box asks you to describe what the specimen submitted consists of—for example, a digitally captured image of the home page where the goods or services are offered, or the front page of an advertisement offering the goods or services for sale.

International Class: Enter the number of the classification you selected for the goods or services offered on your website. (See the instructions for Question 2, above, for more on trademark classifications.) Or, if you prefer, you can send in your application without specifying a class and let the trademark examiner help you. If you want to register under more than one class, click "Form Wizard." This takes you back to the question where you are asked under how many classes you want to register. Once you enter a number other than "one" in that space and click the next button, you will be given a different application template that accommodates multiple classes.

Listing of Goods and/or Services: Here is where you describe the goods or services to which your domain name is attached. The good news is that you are only expected to make your best attempt. A trademark examiner who doesn't approve of your description, or is confused by it, will let you know and work with you to come up with an appropriate description. If you don't feel like guessing, consult the "Trademark Acceptable Identification of Goods and Services Manual," a long list of goods and services that will help you come up with a proper description of the ones you plan to offer on your website. These descriptions are written up by the PTO, so you can copy them directly. You can find this manual online at the Commissioner for Trademarks page of the PTO's website. From the home page, click on the USPTO Organizational Structure icon.

US Patent and Trademark Office

HOME   SITE INDEX   SEARCH   INFO BY ORG   FEEDBACK

Trademark Acceptable Identification
of Goods and Services Manual

Table of Contents

Goods

The **S** field indicates the status of the record: **A**=added, **M**=modified, **D**=deleted. The **Date** field indicates the date of that status. Minor corrections to an entry, e.g., typos, are not considered changes in status.

T	IC	S	Date	Goods
G	009	A	2/20/96	Abacuses
G	010	A	4/2/91	Abdominal belts
G	010	A	4/2/91	Abdominal corsets
G	010	A	4/2/91	Abdominal pads
G	001	A	4/2/91	Abrasive [indicate specific use or industry] (Auxiliary fluids for use with)
G	001	A	4/2/91	Abrasive compositions used in the manufacture of metal polish
G	021	A	1/1/95	Abrasive liners for cat litter boxes
G	007	A	4/2/91	Abrasive wheels (Power operated)
G	005	A	4/2/91	Abrasives (Dental)
G	001	A	4/2/91	Absorbing carbons [indicate specific use or industry]
G	005	A	4/2/91	Acaricides for [indicate specific area of use, e.g., agricultural, commercial, domestic]
G	015	A	4/2/91	Accordions
G	016	A	4/2/91	Account books
G	016	A	4/2/91	Accounting forms
G	005	A	1/1/95	Acetaminophen [for relief of pain]
G	017	A	4/2/91	Acetate, for use in [indicate specific field of use] (Semi-processed cellulose)
G	011	A	4/2/91	Acetylene burners
G	011	A	4/2/91	Acetylene flares
G	009	A	4/2/91	Acid hydrometers
G	029	A	4/2/91	Acidophilus milk
G	005	A	4/2/91	Acne medications
G	005	A	4/2/91	Acne treatment preparations
G	015	A	4/2/91	Acoustic guitars
G	017	A	4/2/91	Acoustical insulation barrier panels
G	017	A	4/2/91	Acoustical insulation for buildings
G	017	A	4/2/91	Acoustical panels for buildings
G	022	A	4/2/91	Acrylic fibers
G	017	A	4/2/91	Acrylic molded plastic substances, for use in [indicate specific field of use] (Semi-finished)
G	017	A	4/2/91	Acrylic resin sheeting for use in the manufacture of laminated glass
G	001	A	4/2/91	Acrylic resins [indicate specific use or industry](Unprocessed)
G	017	A	4/2/91	Acrylic sheeting for use in the manufacture of [indicate specific item]
G	009	A	4/2/91	Actinometers
G	028	A	4/2/91	Action balls (Rubber)
G	028	A	4/2/91	Action figures and accessories therefor
G	028	A	4/2/91	Action figures
G	028	A	4/2/91	Action skill games
G	028	A	4/2/91	Action toys (Mechanical)
G	028	A	4/2/91	Action toys [indicate specific type of operation, e.g., mechanical, electric, etc.]
G	028	A	4/2/91	Action-type target games
G	010	A	7/1/94	Acupuncture instruments [electric or non-electric]
G	010	A	7/1/94	Acupuncture needles
G	016	A	4/2/91	Adding machine paper
G	009	A	4/2/91	Adding machines
G	001	M	3/15/93	Additives (Chemical gasoline)
G	001	M	3/15/93	Additives (Chemical motor oil)
G	001	A	4/2/91	Additives (Concrete)
G	004	A	3/15/93	Additives (Non-chemical gasoline)
G	004	A	3/15/93	Additives (Non-chemical motor oil)
G	031	A	4/2/91	Additives for animal feed (Non medicated)
G	005	A	4/2/91	Additives for livestock feed (Nutritional)
G	030	A	4/2/91	Additives for non-nutritional purposes (Flavoring)
G	031	A	4/2/91	Additives for non-nutritional purposes for use as flavoring, ingredient or filler (Animal feed
G	030	A	4/2/91	Additives for non-nutritional purposes for use as flavoring, ingredient or filler (Food)
G	001	M	3/15/93	Additives for use in the manufacture of [indicate specific items, e.g., good, pharmaceuticals, o
G	001	A	4/2/91	Additives to prevent rust (Radiator)
G	016	A	4/2/91	Address books
G	016	A	4/2/91	Address labels
G	016	A	4/2/91	Address plates
G	016	A	4/2/91	Addressing machines
G	005	A	7/1/94	Adhesive bandages
G	017	A	4/2/91	Adhesive bands for sealing cartons for industrial or commercial use
G	017	A	4/2/91	Adhesive bands for sealing pharmaceutical containers
G	001	A	4/2/91	Adhesive cement for hobbyists
G	016	A	4/2/91	Adhesive dispensers for office use (Automatic)
G	005	A	4/2/91	Adhesive for bandages for skin wounds
G	017	A	4/2/91	Adhesive packing tape for industrial or commercial use

Trademark Acceptable Identification of Goods and Services Manual

Try to make your description as precise as possible. If your description is too broad, it may describe services in more than one class. And remember, each extra class added to your application will cost another $325. The examiner will probably contact you before adding more classes, so it won't be a surprise. But it may delay the processing of your application.

➡ The next two sections relating to dates of first use are for use applicants only. ("Intent to use" applicants should skip down to "Fee Information," below.)

Date of First Use of Mark Anywhere: Here you are asked to provide the date you first started using the unique part of your domain name—the part to the left of the dot. If you have been using it in an existing business, enter the date you first used that name as part of a commercial transaction. If its first use was as a domain name, then your date of first use is the date your website went live to sell goods or services.

Date of First Use of the Mark in Commerce: Enter the date when you first used the unique part of your domain name in commerce across state, territorial or international borders. If you have an existing business, this date may be different than the date of first use that you just entered. For example, you may have first used the name to market your business locally and later gone national or international. The first date would be your use anywhere, and the second date would be the date the scope of your business expanded. If the unique part of your domain name is being used for the first time as your domain name, enter the date of first use.

If you've been using a mark for years and don't remember the exact date of its first use anywhere or across state lines, make your best estimate. Use dated documents that you have gathered over the years, such as old advertisements or business licenses, to help jog your memory. If necessary, use imprecise dates, such as "before March 25, 1998," "on or about January 16, 1975," "in 1966" or "in February 1984." Use the earliest possible date that you can reasonably assert as correct.

Fee Information

Number of Classes: Use the drop-down box to select the number of classes in which you are registering the mark.

Amount: If you are registering in just one class, as most people do, enter $325. The fee will be $325 more for each additional class.

Payment Method: Again, check the credit card box if it isn't already checked from your earlier entry.

Declaration: Read it carefully. If there are statements in the declaration that raise serious doubts or questions in your mind, see a trademark lawyer. (For information about how to find a lawyer, see Chapter 9.)

Signature: The information box right above the signature section provides the surprising information that your "signature," when you file online and don't actually sign any paper, can be whatever you choose. You can enter any combination of letters, numbers or other characters as your "signature." Each signature must begin and end with a forward slash (/). For example, /pat smith/; /ps/; and /268-3421/ are all acceptable signatures. There's no trick here. Unless you've developed some special internal system for tracking electronic signatures in your office, entering your own name is the simplest option. Click the signature link just below the information box for the PTO's own words on this subject.

Validate: This process checks your application and alerts you if you forgot to include any information that is mandatory. You will then have a chance to go back and fill in the missing information. A warning message will also appear for non-mandatory missing information, but you are not required to go back and include that information. Once the validation is done, click "Pay/Submit" at the bottom of the Validation screen. Since you are using a credit card for payment, you will next be asked to enter payment information. If your transaction is successful, you will receive a confirmation screen.

Later, you will receive an email acknowledging the submission of your application. Hold on to that email, because it is the only proof you'll have that the PTO has your application. It is also proof of your filing date and contains the serial number assigned to your application.

E. What Happens Next

If you filed a "use" application, you will likely receive some communication from the PTO within three to six months. If there is a problem with your application, you will receive what's called an "action letter." This is simply a letter from your examiner explaining what the problems are. Most problems can be resolved with a phone call to the examiner.

When the examiner approves your application for publication, you will receive a Notice of Publication in the mail. Your mark will then be published in the *Official Gazette* (a PTO journal) for 30 days. During that time, anyone may oppose your registration. Only 3% of all published marks are opposed, so it is unlikely you will run into trouble.

Once your mark has made it through the 30-day publication period, you will receive a Certificate of Registration. The PTO has lately had a difficult time moving applications through this long process. As a result, it may take a year or more to process your application.

If you filed on an "intent to use" basis, you will need to file an additional document with the PTO when you start using your domain name. This document is called "Statement of Use/Amendment to Allege Use for Intent-to-Use Application." It tells the PTO the date you started using the domain name and completes the registration process. You must also provide a specimen at that time, showing how you are using the domain name. You can use e-TEAS to file this form as well.

Down the road, you will need to do a few things to keep your registration in force. For example, between five and six years after the mark is first registered, you'll need to file a document stating that you are still using the mark. And your registration must be renewed every ten years; otherwise it will be automatically cancelled. You can use e-TEAS for all these forms. ■

CHAPTER 9

Help Beyond This Book

W e hope this book provides all the information you need to register and protect your domain name. But somewhere along the line, you may need additional help. This chapter covers how to get that help from a lawyer or from your own legal research.

If you're looking for information about trademark issues beyond domain names—for example, sorting out trademark disputes or building on your domain name trademark using graphics, packaging, color or product design—then you will want to read *Trademark: Legal Care for Your Business & Product Name*, by Stephen Elias (Nolo). It offers comprehensive coverage of trademark law and trademark searching. To find out more about this book, visit http://www.nolo.com.

A. Domain Name Disputes

There is really no such thing as a domain name dispute, because each domain name is unique—different from every other domain name. What's known as a domain name dispute is a wrangle between a domain name registrant and the owner of a trademark with which the domain name allegedly conflicts. Throughout this book, we have provided guidance on how these types of disputes are likely to be resolved under general trademark principles, the Anti-Cybersquatting Consumer Protection Act of 1999 and ICANN's dispute resolution procedure. Additional guidance is available on the ICANN website as described in Chapter 5, Section D2. By browsing these decisions, you will be able to get a real-world feel for what might happen in your particular dispute. You can also consult Sections B and C, below, which discuss how to research trademark law and keep up to date on developments in trademark law and domain names.

B. Trademark Registration Problems

If you file an electronic trademark application (see Chapter 8), you may find you need more help if, for example:

- You filed your trademark application on an "intent to use" basis and now need guidance on the follow-up documents to complete your registration or obtain a six-month extension for filing them.
- You filed your trademark application, and the PTO staff has told you there is a problem with it or that they need additional information.
- You received a certificate of trademark registration for your domain name (congratulations!), but now need guidance on how to maintain your trademark and keep it registered.

For help with these issues, we suggest these resources:

Trademark: Legal Care for Your Business & Product Name, by Stephen Elias (Nolo). This book explains the procedures and forms for filing all of the forms necessary to complete the trademark application process and keep the registration in effect. You can find out more about this book at http://www.nolo.com.

Handling Problems With Your Trademark Application, by Stephen Elias and Patti Gima. This e-guide, available on the Nolo site in downloadable format, provides detailed guidance on how to respond to the Patent and Trademark Office in the event your application hits a snag.

The *Trademark Manual of Examining Procedure,* the PTO's own manual for evaluating trademark applications, is the bible for trademark examiners, the PTO attorneys who look over your application and ultimately approve or reject your domain name for registration. Virtually every statement they make to you about your application or registration will come with a reference to this publication. You can find this manual at http://www.uspto.gov. Click Trademark, and then click "Trademark Manual of Examining Procedure."

Also, federal trademark law, cases and regulations. If you use the *Trademark Manual of Examining Procedure*, you may find it useful to look up sections of the statute on which the manual's rules are based as well as cases and regulations. See Section C, below, for tips on this process.

C. Doing Your Own Legal Research

Finding information about the law and ferreting out answers to legal questions is called legal research. If you have a question and can't find the answer in a Nolo book on trademarks or the PTO's website, you may want to do your own legal research.

When it comes to addressing such cutting-edge issues as domain name and trademark conflicts, the Internet is the legal research tool of choice. This section gives you an introduction to conducting legal research online. You'll follow these six steps:

1. Find and read the most relevant federal law (statutes).
2. Make sure the law you find is up to date.
3. Find and read relevant regulations issued by the PTO or other agency.
4. Find any court decisions that interpret the relevant statutes and regulations.
5. Read through summaries of the court decisions to find the most relevant case—one that deals with roughly the same facts and issues as your situation.
6. Make sure the court decisions you find are up-to-date.

Legal Research: How to Find & Understand the Law, by Stephen Elias and Susan Levinkind (Nolo), will give you a much more detailed discussion of how to do legal research online and in the law library. It covers the whole process in detail and includes step-by-step instructions for using online research services discussed in this chapter, such as versuslaw.com and keycite.com.

SOME KEY LEGAL TERMS

Statute: A written law passed by Congress or a state legislature and signed into law by the President or a governor. Statutes are often gathered into compilations called "codes," large sets of books that can be found in many public and all law libraries. The federal statutes and the statutes of almost all states are now also available on the Internet.

Case: A term that most often refers to a lawsuit—for example, "I filed my small claims case." However, in our discussion of legal research, "case" refers to a written decision by a trial judge—or, if the trial court's ruling has been appealed, by a panel of appellate judges.

Regulation: A rule that is made by an administrative agency such as the IRS or the PTO. For example, PTO regulations govern the procedures by which trademark applications are filed.

---

1. Find the Most Relevant and Current Federal Statutes

Because domain names are used across state borders, domain name disputes are usually governed by federal laws. A federal statute that talks about the issue you're interested in is generally the best place to start your research.

Federal trademark laws are collectively known both as the Lanham Act and as the Federal Trademark Act of 1946 (as amended). The Lanham Act is codified (published) in Title 15, Sections 1051 through 1127, of the United States Code. There are two versions of the United States Code online—one maintained by Cornell Law School and the other by the House of Representatives Law Library. You can access both of these at Nolo's website.

If you know the specific citation of the statute, you will use the House of Representatives Law Library version. For instance, suppose you are looking for the law dealing with trademark dilution, and know that its citation is Title 15, Section 1125 (perhaps you found the citation in some background material you read). You would take these steps:

- Go to http://www.nolo.com. Scroll down to the Legal Research Center. Click on U.S. Laws and Regulations.
- Scroll down to the U.S. Code part of the page.
- Enter 15 in the Title box and the section number (for instance 1125) in the section box. Click search.

If you don't have a specific citation, the Cornell site is probably your best bet. For instance, assume that you want to find the federal remedies for trademark infringement. You would take these steps to get to and use the Cornell site:

- Follow the first direction above to get to Nolo's U.S. Laws and Regulations page.
- Scroll down to the U.S. Code part of the page.
- Click "Browse the U.S. Code at Cornell Law School."
- Click "Title 15" on the home page first if you want to conduct a keyword search of the Lanham Act for "infringement remedies."
- Alternatively, click "Title 15," scroll down the list of chapters until you get to trademarks (Chapter 22), click that link and browse the subject titles. In this example you would find the statute on infringement remedies in Section 1114.

Both sites offer online searching help if you get stuck.

2. Make Sure You're Reading the Latest Version of the Statute

Once you find the statute and section you're looking for, the next step is to make sure the version you're looking at is current. Laws change, and it does you little good to look over a law that is outdated. It takes a lot of time to update the United States Code, and you may be searching a version of the U.S. Code that is really two years out-of-date.

For updating federal statutes, we recommend the Thomas website, at http://thomas.loc.gov. This site provides both pending and recently enacted legislation. Follow the instructions carefully to see whether a particular statute you've found in the code has been amended or even repealed by more recent legislation.

Thomas also helps you research all bills pending before Congress as well as bills recently passed and signed into law by the President. Keeping track of pending bills will give you a leg up on the most recent changes to the U.S. Code should those bills eventually become law. The information on Thomas is organized according to the session of Congress you are searching for—for example, the 106th Congress (1998-1999). If you don't know which period of time you are interested in, you will need to search each session that might be important. Searches in Thomas can be made by topic, by a bill's popular title or by bill number. Finally you can search by public law number—for instance, P.L. 96-4537. The public law number is how a statute is identified until it is placed with other statutes of similar subject matter in the United States Code.

3. Find Relevant Federal Regulations

If you decide to register your domain name as a trademark with the U.S. Patent and Trademark Office (see Chapter 8), you may have occasion to study the trademark rules issued by the PTO. As mentioned, these rules are known as regulations and are published in Title 37, Chapter 1, of the

Code of Federal Regulations (C.F.R.). There are two reasons why you would want to look up PTO regulations:

- The PTO refers to a particular regulation when corresponding with you, or on its website.
- You are trying to figure out what a particular statute means and wish to see whether the PTO has interpreted it.

You can find these regulations via Nolo's website by taking the following steps:

- Go to http://www.nolo.com and scroll down to the Legal Research Center. Click on U.S. Code and Regulations.
- Scroll down to find the Code of Federal Regulations and enter a keyword or section number. Trademark regulations are found in Title 37, Parts 1-199, Section 2.

4. Find Relevant Court Decisions

If you are trying to answer a legal question, you not only need to know what the underlying laws say, you also need to know what the courts have had to say on your particular issue. Court decisions make up what we call the "common law." As a general rule, the higher the court deciding the case, the more important the case is. The U.S. Supreme Court always has the last word on federal laws.

THE FEDERAL COURT SYSTEM

The federal court system has three tiers. Federal District Courts, the trial courts of the federal system, hear lawsuits for the first time. Certain cases are heard in specialized federal trial courts, such as bankruptcy court or tax court. On the second level are the federal Courts of Appeal, which hear appeals from the District Courts. An appeal is a process by which one party to a lawsuit (usually the losing party) asks a higher court to review the actions of a lower court to correct mistakes or injustice. On the top level is the United States Supreme Court, which hears appeals in a few select cases of its choosing.

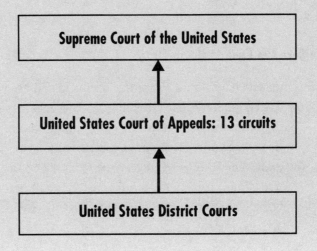

If you have found a relevant statute or regulation, your next best step is to look for court decisions that have interpreted it. The best way to do this is to search for the statute, by number, in a database of court decisions. There are several such databases online. Dollar for dollar, we prefer Versuslaw at http://www.versuslaw.com. This service costs $6.95 a month and gives you access to most state and federal court decisions. Online help is readily available.

One site in particular does a good job of collecting domain name and trademark cases and providing commentary on what they mean to this rapidly developing legal area.

www.phillipsnizer.com This site, maintained by a New York law firm, offers the best collection of cases dealing with domain name disputes. It provides both a brief and an extensive summary for each case, and a link to the full text of the case if it is available online. When you get to the home page, first click "Internet Library" and then "Domain Name/Path." The cases are listed in alphabetical order. The more cases you read on this subject, the better feel you'll have for how a court would likely rule in yours if you end up in court.

5. Make Sure the Case Is Up-to-Date

Once you have found a case that seems to address your question, you will need to check that it is still good law. A case is still "good law" if it hasn't been overruled or modified by a more recent case. The best way to do a check online is to use a tool called KeyCite at http:// www.keycite.com. KeyCite costs $3.75 a search (a credit card is required), but it usually takes only one search to find out whether or not the case you found is still good law. KeyCite comes with online help.

D. Finding a Lawyer

If you become involved in a domain name dispute, are having trouble getting your mark registered or simply want some advice from a professional, you may want to consult a lawyer—but not just any lawyer. Start by understanding that if you have read substantial portions of this book you already know more about domain names and trademarks than most lawyers do. This puts you in the difficult position of finding someone who knows more than you do and yet is willing to acknowledge your considerable competence.

We know of no sure-fire way to find such a rare creature, but here are what we think are some good suggestions.

1. Finding a Competent Lawyer

Trademark lawyers (including those who specialize in domain name issues) usually advertise in the Yellow Pages and legal journals as intellectual property specialists, able to handle patent, trademark, copyright and trade secret cases. State and local bar associations may also keep rosters of intellectual property attorneys. Such ads and listings can be misleading because most intellectual property law specialists tend to be very knowledgeable in one or two areas of intellectual property, and only passingly familiar with the others.

You want a lawyer who really knows trademark law as it pertains to domain names, not just someone willing to brush up on the subject at your expense. So when you call on the intellectual property specialist, ask these questions:

- Do you have experience with domain name disputes? If so, what types of disputes have you been involved in? Any experience with domain name litigation (taking a case to court) or ICANN dispute procedures?
- What percentage of your practice involves domain name disputes?
- How many applications have you filed with the PTO to register domain names as trademarks?
- Are you a member of the International Trademark Association or the American Intellectual Property Law Association?

The first three questions will help you find a true specialist in this area, while the fourth will help you find a lawyer who is involved enough with trademark issues to join an association of trademark specialists.

2. Finding a Respectful Lawyer

In addition to satisfying yourself that a lawyer is competent, you want to find someone who is reasonably congenial to work with. You don't need us to tell you that many lawyers tend to look down on laypersons when it comes to the lawyer's area of expertise. This means that many of the lawyers you initially encounter are likely to be turned off by your knowledge. Fortunately, however, some lawyers respect their clients' knowledge and know how to work with it rather than against it.

You can find a lawyer who isn't intimidated by a competent client if you:

- explain over the phone that you have been using this book
- articulate exactly what you want the lawyer to do; and
- carefully monitor the lawyer's reaction.

If the lawyer scoffs at the idea of a self-help law book or you get a whiff of, "Don't tell me what you need, I'm the lawyer," go on to the next name on the list. If the response appears to respect your efforts to educate yourself and admits to the possibility that you are a competent human being, make an appointment.

3. Finding an Honest and Conscientious Lawyer

If you are just seeking advice, then you needn't worry much about the lawyer's character. But if you are looking for someone to represent you, the human being you are dealing with becomes paramount. The best analytical trademark lawyer in the world can bring you to financial and emotional ruin, if he or she lacks the ability to understand your needs and to represent you with your best interests in mind.

a. Honesty

A lawyer's financial interest—to run up lots of billable hours over a period of time—is the opposite of yours, which is to arrive at a fast, cost-efficient and reasonably livable resolution of the problem.

Once you understand this, you'll also understand that it is essential that you and your lawyer agree up front about what the lawyer is to do and the amount of control you are to have over the lawyer's activities. Rule One is that the lawyer is working for you, not vice versa. Rule Two is that you have a right to understand the reason for every minute of the lawyer's time that will be billed to you. To make sure you're at least informed about the lawyer's activities and how much you're being charged for them, always ask for a signed agreement between you and your lawyer setting out the lawyer's fees and stating that the lawyer will send you an itemized bill each month. An honest fee agreement will also list all costs that you will be charged for—faxes, photocopies, courier fees and overnight mail fees, for example.

b. Conscientiousness

Your lawyer must be willing to agree to consult you regularly on all phases of the case and to promptly return your phone calls. Although nothing leads to a ruinous relationship faster than bad communication, too few lawyers keep their clients well-posted. Lawyers faced with complaints about their lousy client contact habits often reply that many clients call too often or expect too much. But since the client is paying for the lawyer's time, this seems like a pretty weak excuse.

Your lawyer must also be willing to follow through on your case to its completion. He or she must be ready to stay involved and on top of your case no matter how rocky it gets. For example, if a settlement is expected at the outset, but the case ends up going to court, your lawyer must be willing to go the distance with you and not back out at the last minute. This one is tricky to monitor, because it involves predicting the future. However, as long as good communication is established at the outset, there's an improved chance that your lawyer will give you reliable service. ■

Appendices

APPENDIX A: GLOSSARY

APPENDIX B: INTERNATIONAL SCHEDULE OF CLASSES OF GOODS
   AND SERVICES

APPENDIX C: IDENTIFICATION AND CLASSIFICATION OF CERTAIN
   COMPUTER-RELATED GOODS AND SERVICES

Appendix A

Glossary

abandonment loss of trademark rights resulting from nonuse of mark and demonstrated by sufficient evidence that the owner intends to discontinue use of the mark; may also occur when mark has lost its distinctiveness or through owner's misuse of trademark rights.

ACCPA the Anti-Cybersquatting Consumer Protection Act, a federal statute which prohibits cybersquatting. Under the Act, cybersquatting is defined as registering, trafficking in or using a domain name with a bad-faith intent to profit from the goodwill of a trademark belonging to someone else.

actual use use of a mark in a bona fide commercial transaction to identify the underlying product or service. A trademark is put into actual use when it is attached to the product it identifies; a service mark is deemed to be in actual use when it is used or displayed in the sale or advertising of commercial services. The first to make actual use of a mark is considered its owner.

arbitrary mark a word or group of words that has a dictionary meaning that does not pertain to the goods or services with which it is associated.

assignment a permanent transfer of trademark rights and goodwill.

blurring a form of dilution in which a famous mark loses some of its distinctiveness due to the use of a similar mark.

certification mark a mark that indicates that third party goods and services meet certain standards such as regional origin, material, mode of manufacture, quality, accuracy, or that the work or labor was performed by a member of a certain organization.

collective mark used by members of a cooperative, an association or other collective group or organization to indicate membership or to indicate the source of the organization's products or services.

commerce for purposes of protection of U.S. trademarks, any trade or business lawfully regulated by the United States.

common law a system of legal rules derived from the precedents and principles established by court decisions.

concurrent use a legal determination that more than one person is entitled to use a similar mark.

counterfeiting the act of making or selling look-alike goods or services bearing fake trademarks.

cybersquatter a person who registers a well-known trademark as a domain name hoping to later profit by selling the domain name to the trademark owner.

defamation of business false statements that injure a business's reputation. Defamation affects the manner in which the public perceives the company's trademarked products.

descriptive mark a name or term that merely describes a product or service (or its nature, quality, characteristics, ingredients or origin). A descriptive mark is considered as "weak."

dilution a form of trademark injury that occurs when a famous mark's reputation is blurred or tarnished by the commercial use of a similar mark. Unlike traditional trademark infringement, there is no requirement of consumer confusion, and the parties do not have to be competitors selling similar goods or services.

disclaimer a trademark owner's statement that he or she asserts no exclusive right in a specific portion of a mark, apart from its use within the mark.

disparagement false statements that interfere with a company's business relations and negatively affect a company's ability to do business.

distinctive mark a mark that is immediately distinguishable such as an arbitrary, fanciful, suggestive mark.

domain name an identifier of a website location consisting of two parts; a generic top-level domain (such as .com or .org) and a second level that is the name of the business or organization (such as amazon or eBay). A domain name is also a trademark or service mark if it is used to identify commercial activity on the associated website.

drawing a substantially exact representation of the mark in use or (in the case of intent-to-use applications) as intended to be used. A drawing is required for all federal trademark applications and for many state trademark applications.

fair use a defense to trademark infringement in which a trademark is used in a descriptive manner, rather than as a source of goods.

fanciful marks a word or a combination of letters that has no dictionary meaning and for that reason is immediately distinctive.

generic term a term that describes an entire group or class of goods.

genericide the process by which trademark rights are lost because consumers have begun to think of the trademark as the descriptive name for the goods; results from a judicial determination or inter partes proceeding at the Patent and Trademark Office.

geographic composite mark a mark composed of a geographic term with additional wording or a design, for example, *Bell Atlantic*.

geographically descriptive (weak) a geographic term that describes the origin, location or source of the product or service (for example, *First National Bank of Bloomington* for a bank located in Bloomington, Indiana).

geographically misdescriptive (unprotectible) a geographic term that misleads consumers into believing that the product originates from a region when it does not. For example, *Danish Maid Cultured Products* is geographically misdescriptive of products that were not from Denmark.

goodwill the tendency or likelihood of a consumer to repurchase goods or services based upon the name or source of the goods or services.

ICANN the International Corporation for Assigned Names and Numbers, the international non-profit group in charge of Internet domain name policy.

incontestable a trademark that is immune from challenge except for certain grounds specified in Section 33(b) of the Lanham Act; conclusive evidence of the registrant's exclusive right to use the registered mark in commerce in connection with the specified goods or services. A mark becomes incontestable if it remains on the federal principal trademark register for at least five years, and the owner files the proper documents.

infringement occurs when the junior user's goods or services create a likelihood of confusion with the senior user's goods or services.

inherently distinctive see *distinctive mark.*

injunction a court order directing the defendant to stop certain activities.

intellectual property any product of the human mind that is protectible under law.

intent-to-use an application for federal trademark registration based upon the trademark owner's bona fide intention to use the mark in commerce. If the mark is put into actual use and the owner completes the registration process, the date the intent-to-use application was filed is considered the date of first use.

inter partes a formal administrative hearing governed by federal rules of civil procedure and evidence.

interference proceeding a mini-trial before the Trademark Trial and Appeal Board brought when two trademark applications are pending that conflict, or when a pending application conflicts with a registered mark that is not incontestable; only permitted under extraordinary circumstances.

international schedule of classes of goods and services a system for classification of goods and services applicable to federal trademark applications filed on or after September 1, 1973.

junior user a party who adopts and uses a trademark similar to a mark previously adopted and used by a senior user.

laches a defense to infringement in which the junior user argues that the senior user's delay in bringing the lawsuit is so unreasonable that the senior user should be barred from proceeding.

likelihood of confusion when the facts make it likely that consumers would mistake one product or service for another or be confused as to their source. A likelihood of confusion provides a basis for a finding of infringement, prevents the federal registration of a mark and may determine the outcome of an inter partes proceeding.

merely descriptive see *descriptive mark.*

opposition proceeding an action brought before the Trademark Trial and Appeal Board to prevent the federal registration of a mark; must be based upon one of the statutory grounds provided in the Lanham Act and the party bringing the action must prove that it would be damaged.

parody a defense used by a junior user who seeks to justify its imitation on the premise of humor or satirical social commentary. As a general rule, the same likelihood of confusion standards are applied in a case involving parody as in any other type of infringement. The difference is that the junior user attempts to argue that consumers could not be confused because the use is obviously a joke.

permanent injunction a court order issued after a final judgment on the merits of the case; permanently restrains the defendant from engaging in the infringing activity.

preliminary injunction a court order granted after a noticed hearing where the parties have an opportunity to present evidence as to the likelihood of plaintiff's success on the merits and irreparability of the harm to be suffered if the injunction is not granted; lasts until a final judgment has been rendered.

priority a senior user's right to prevent a junior user from using a mark.

related goods or services goods or services that the consuming public is likely to encounter in the same marketing channels.

remedies forms of judicial relief available in a lawsuit, such as damages, injunctions and attorney fees.

reverse confusion an infringement situation in which the junior user is more well-known than the senior user; often creates the impression that the senior user is infringing the junior user.

secondary meaning demonstration that the consuming public associates a mark with a single source; usually proved by advertising, promotion and sales.

second-level domain name (SLD) the portion of a domain name before the "dot," such as "nolo" in nolo.com.

senior user the first party to adopt and use a particular mark in connection with its goods or services.

service mark a mark used in the sale or advertising of services to identify and distinguish services; treated the same as a trademark for all practical purposes.

strong mark a mark entitled to much trademark protection, achieved by an inherently distinctive mark or by a nondistinctive mark that has achieved secondary meaning.

suggestive mark a mark that alludes to or hints at (without describing) the nature or quality of the goods; considered a legally strong mark entitled to legal protection from copiers.

tarnishment a form of dilution that occurs when a famous mark is damaged by an unpleasant or unwholesome use of a similar mark.

temporary restraining order (TRO) an injunction, often granted *ex parte*, that is short in duration and only remains in effect until the court has an opportunity to schedule a hearing for a preliminary injunction.

top-level domain name (TLD) the generic portion of a domain name after the "dot." The currently operable TLDs are .com (commercial entities), .net (interactive groups), .org (organizations), .gov (government) and .edu (educational institutions). TLDs approved by ICANN but not yet in use are .aero (airtransport), .biz (businesses), .coop (nonprofits), .info (unrestricted), .museum (museums), .name (individuals) and .pro (accountants, lawyers and physicians).

trade dress a distinctive packaging or combination of visual elements that collectively identify the source of a product or service; protected by federal trademark law although individual aspects of the overall trade dress may not be protectible.

trademark any word, symbol, design, device, logo or slogan that identifies and distinguishes one product or service from another.

unfair competition a collection of common law principles and precedents, many of which are adopted as state laws, that protect against unethical business practices.

Uniform Domain Name Dispute Resolution Policy (UDRP) an international system sponsored by ICANN that requires all domain name holders to submit to arbitration if their right to use their domain names is challenged by a trademark owner; the arbitration can result in the loss of the domain name if the domain name registrant is shown to have registered or used the name in bad faith.

URL (Uniform Resource Locator) a system for locating a website; generally begins with http://www. followed by a domain name.

use in commerce a statutory term meaning any use of the mark in the type of commerce that the federal government has authority to regulate; usually commerce between states or between states and foreign countries, but also any activity that affects interstate commerce, such as a major resort destination like Disney World. Use in commerce is a requirement for federal registration and protection of a mark.

utility patent legal protection granted for inventions or discoveries that are machines, processes, compositions, articles of manufacture or new uses of any of these.

weak mark nondistinctive names or terms that cannot be registered or protected as a trademark unless the owner proves a consumer awareness or "secondary meaning." ∎

Appendix B

International Schedule of Classes of Goods and Services

Goods

1. Chemical products used in industry, science, photography, agriculture, horticulture, forestry; artificial and synthetic resins; plastics in the form of powders, liquids or pastes, for industrial use; manures (natural and artificial); fire extinguishing compositions; tempering substances and chemical preparations for soldering; chemical substances for preserving foodstuffs; tanning substances; adhesive substances used in industry.

2. Paints, varnishes, lacquers; preservatives against rust and against deterioration of wood; colouring matters, dyestuffs; mordants; natural resins; metals in foil and powder form for painters and decorators.

3. Bleaching preparations and other substances for laundry use; cleaning, polishing, scouring and abrasive preparations; soaps; perfumery, essential oils, cosmetics, hair lotions; dentifrices.

4. Industrial oils and greases (other than oils and fats and essential oils); lubricants; dust laying and absorbing compositions; fuels (including motor spirit) and illuminants; candles, tapers, night lights and wicks.

5. Pharmaceutical, veterinary, and sanitary substances; infants' and invalids' foods; plasters, material for bandaging; material for stopping teeth, dental wax, disinfectants; preparations for killing weeds and destroying vermin.

6. Unwrought and partly wrought common metals and their alloys; anchors, anvils, bells, rolled and cast building materials; rails and other metallic materials for railway tracks; chains (except driving

chains for vehicles); cables and wires (nonelectric); locksmiths' work; metallic pipes and tubes; safes and cash boxes; steel balls; horseshoes; nails and screws; other goods in nonprecious metal not included in other classes; ores.

7. Machines and machine tools; motors (except for land vehicles); machine couplings and belting (except for land vehicles); large size agricultural implements; incubators.

8. Hand tools and instruments; cutlery, forks and spoons; side arms.

9. Scientific, nautical, surveying and electrical apparatus and instruments (including wireless), photographic, cinematographic, optical, weighing, measuring, signalling, checking (supervision), life-saving and teaching apparatus and instruments; coin or counterfreed apparatus; talking machines; cash registers; calculating machines; fire extinguishing apparatus.

10. Surgical, medical, dental, and veterinary instruments and apparatus (including artificial limbs, eyes and teeth).

11. Installations for lighting, heating, steam generating, cooking, refrigerating, drying, ventilating, water supply, and sanitary purposes.

12. Vehicles; apparatus for locomotion by land, air or water.

13. Firearms; ammunition and projectiles; explosive substances; fireworks.

14. Precious metals and their alloys and goods in precious metals or coated therewith (except cutlery forks and spoons); jewelry, precious stones, horological and other chronometric instruments.

15. Musical instruments (other than talking machines and wireless apparatus).

16. Paper and paper articles, cardboard and cardboard articles; printed matter, newspaper and periodicals, books; bookbinding material; photographs; stationery, adhesive materials (stationery): artists' materials; paint brushes; typewriters and office requisites (other than furniture); instructional and teaching material (other than apparatus); playing cards; printers' type and cliches (stereotype).

17. Gutta percha, india rubber, balata and substitutes, articles made from these substances and not included in other classes; plastics in the form of sheets, blocks and rods, being for use in manufacture; materials for packing, stopping or insulating; asbestos, mica and their products; hose pipes (nonmetallic).

18. Leather and imitations of leather, and articles made from these materials and not included in other classes; skins, hides; trunks and travelling bags; umbrellas, parasols and walking sticks; whips, harness and saddlery.

19. Building materials, natural and artificial stone, cement, lime, mortar, plaster and gravel; pipes or earthenware or cement; roadmaking materials; asphalt, pitch and bitumen; portable buildings; stone monuments; chimney pots.

20. Furniture, mirrors, picture frames; articles (not included in other classes) of wood, cork, reeds, cane, wicker, horn, bone, ivory, whalebone, shell, amber, mother-of-pearl, meerschaum, celluloid, substitutes for all these materials, or of plastics.

21. Small domestic utensils and containers (not of precious metals, or coated therewith); combs and sponges; brushes (other than paint brushes); brushmaking materials; instruments and material for cleaning purposes, steel wool; unworked or semi-worked glass (excluding glass used in building); glassware, porcelain and earthenware, not included in other classes.

22. Ropes, string, nets, tents, awnings, tarpaulins, sails, sacks; padding and stuffing materials (hair, kapok, feathers, seaweed, etc.); raw fibrous textile materials.

23. Yarns, threads.

24. Tissues (piece goods); bed and table covers; textile articles not included in other classes.

25. Clothing, including boots, shoes and slippers.

26. Lace and embroidery, ribbons and braid; buttons, press buttons, hooks and eyes, pins and needles; artificial flowers.

27. Carpets, rugs, mats and matting; linoleums and other materials for covering existing floors; wall hangings (nontextile).

28. Games and playthings; gymnastic and sporting articles (except clothing); ornaments and decorations for Christmas trees.

29. Meats, fish, poultry and game; meat extracts; preserved, dried and cooked fruits and vegetables; jellies, jams; eggs, milk and other dairy products; edible oils and fats; preserves, pickles.

30. Coffee, tea, cocoa, sugar, rice, tapioca, sago, coffee substitutes; flour, and preparations made from cereals; bread, biscuits, cakes, pastry and confectionery, ices; honey, treacle; yeast, baking powder; salt, mustard, pepper, vinegar, sauces, spices; ice.

31. Agricultural, horticultural and forestry products and grains not included in other classes; living animals; fresh fruits and vegetables; seeds; live plants and flowers; foodstuffs for animals, malt.

32. Beer, ale and porter; mineral and aerated waters and other nonalcoholic drinks; syrups and other preparations for making beverages.

33. Wines, spirits and liqueurs.

34. Tobacco, raw or manufactured; smokers' articles; machines.

Services

35. Advertising and business.

36. Insurance and financial.

37. Construction and repair.

38. Communication.

39. Transportation and Storage.

40. Material treatment.

41. Education and entertainment.

42. Miscellaneous.

Appendix C

Identification and Classification of Certain Computer-Related Goods and Services

Class 9:

Pre-recorded software on CD-ROMs, diskettes, magnetic tapes, etc. is in Class 9. The description must provide an indication of the subject matter or function of the software and the subject matter or function indication must be detailed and specific. Very broad statements of function such as "computer programs for business use" are not acceptable.

Class 9:

Computer software [specify the function of the programs, e.g., for use in data base management, for use as a spreadsheet, for word processing, etc.] that is downloaded from a remote computer site" is classified in Class 9.

NOTE: This is a change in classification policy. Previously, "downloadable computer software" was being classified in International Class 42. After a review of this policy, the PTO has decided to classify downloadable software in Class 9 with other software. The placement of downloadable software in International Class 9 is consistent with the practice in a number of other countries.

Class 16:

Only hard copy publications, e.g., printed magazines and books, are considered to be Class 16 goods.

NOTE: Magazines or books that are downloadable from a computer network are not considered to be "hard goods" and they are classified in International Class 42, rather than Class 16. The service is defined as providing the publications on a global computer network and the subject matter of the publications must be specified. If an entire magazine or other publication is presented at the web site, the computer service of providing that publication electronically is considered to be the primary service involved in this activity. The service being provided is that of making available magazines, books and/or other publications via a computer. Appropriate language for these services would be: "Computer services, namely, providing on-line [indicate specific nature of the publication] in the field of [indicate subject matter of the publication]" in Class 42. As with Class 16 publications, the subject matter of the publication does not affect the classification of this service.

Classes 35, 36, 37, 39, 40 & 41:

Any activity consisting of a service that ordinarily falls in these classes (e.g. computer games, various financial transactions, etc.) that also happens to be provided by means of a global computer network, is classified in the class where the underlying service is classified. For example, banking services are in Class 36 whether provided in a bank or on-line by means of global computer network. Similarly, the service of providing information by means of a global computer network is classified in the class of the information subject. Entities who offer these services by computer are considered "content providers," that is, they provide the information or substantive content for a web site and/or home page. A recitation of services for these specific content providers should read "providing information in the field of…by means of a global computer network." The service would be classified by the class of the subject matter of the information. If an entity provides information in a wide variety of fields, this must be reflected in the identification and the service may be classified in Class 42 (e.g., providing information in a wide variety of fields by means of a global computer information network.) Please note that the term "access" should be reserved for use in recitations for network service providers, such as, America OnLine®, Prodigy® and CompuServe®. The PTO considers the use of the term "access" by a content provider to be inaccurate because it causes confusion with the service provider activities.

These guidelines also apply to activities in Classes 38 and 42, however, the comments below also apply to Classes 38 and 42.

Class 38:

The service of providing telecommunications connections to a global computer network is classified in Class 38. These services are purely telecommunications "connections" such as those provided by AT&T®, MCI® or other telecommunications providers. It is ONLY the technical means by which one computer can communicate with another. The telecommunications provider does NOT provide the computer hardware that stores and processes the date: it provides the means by which data is transferred. This service connects the user to the "link provider" (see Class 42 discussion below) or the web site itself.

Class 42:

The service of providing multiple-user access to a global computer information network for the transfer and dissemination of a wide range of information is classified in International Class 42. This language covers those services provided by entities such as America OnLine®, Prodigy® and CompuServe®. They provide the computer service (often using the telecommunications services of other entities as described above in Class 38) that enable computer users to access data bases and home pages of others. These entities are considered "link providers" in that they provide the computer/server connection required for computer users to access a content provider. The word "access" should be limited to these services and should not be used in describing the service of a content provider.

NOTE: A single entity may provide one or more of the services described above. However, each service must be properly identified and classified.

General Comment:

The term "Internet" is still the subject of a proceeding at the Trademark Trial and Appeal Board. Therefore, this term should not be used in identifying any goods or services connected with a global computer information network. Language such as "global computer information network" or a substantive equivalent should be used instead of the term "Internet." ■

INDEX

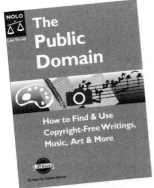

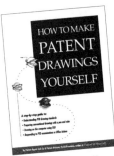

Take 2 minutes & Give us your 2 cents

Your comments make a big difference in the development and revision of Nolo books and software. Please take a few minutes and register your Nolo product—and your comments—with us. Not only will your input make a difference, you'll receive special offers available only to registered owners of Nolo products on our newest books and software. Register now by:

PHONE
1-800-992-6656

FAX
1-800-645-0895

EMAIL
cs@nolo.com

or **MAIL** us
this registration card

REMEMBER:
Little publishers have big ears. We really listen to you.

fold here

REGISTRATION CARD

NAME _____ DATE _____

ADDRESS _____

_____

CITY _____ STATE _____ ZIP _____

PHONE _____ E-MAIL _____

WHERE DID YOU HEAR ABOUT THIS PRODUCT? _____

WHERE DID YOU PURCHASE THIS PRODUCT? _____

DID YOU CONSULT A LAWYER? (PLEASE CIRCLE ONE)   YES   NO   NOT APPLICABLE

DID YOU FIND THIS BOOK HELPFUL?   (VERY)   5   4   3   2   1   (NOT AT ALL)

COMMENTS _____

_____

_____

WAS IT EASY TO USE?   (VERY EASY)   5   4   3   2   1   (VERY DIFFICULT)

DO YOU OWN A COMPUTER? IF SO, WHICH FORMAT? (PLEASE CIRCLE ONE)   WINDOWS   DOS   MAC

We occasionally make our mailing list available to carefully selected companies whose products may be of interest to you.
❑ If you do not wish to receive mailings from these companies, please check this box.
❑ You can quote me in future Nolo promotional materials. Daytime phone number _____.

DOM 2.0

NOLO IN THE NEWS

"Nolo helps lay people perform legal tasks without the aid—or fees—of lawyers."

—**USA TODAY**

Nolo books are ..."written in plain language, free of legal mumbo jumbo, and spiced with witty personal observations."

—**ASSOCIATED PRESS**

"...Nolo publications...guide people simply through the how, when, where and why of law."

—**WASHINGTON POST**

"Increasingly, people who are not lawyers are performing tasks usually regarded as legal work... And consumers, using books like Nolo's, do routine legal work themselves."

—**NEW YORK TIMES**

"...All of [Nolo's] books are easy-to-understand, are updated regularly, provide pull-out forms...and are often quite moving in their sense of compassion for the struggles of the lay reader."

—**SAN FRANCISCO CHRONICLE**

fold here

- -

nolo
950 Parker Street
Berkeley, CA 94710-9867

Attn: ┌─────────────┐
         │ **DOM 2.0** │
         └─────────────┘